MA HUATENG

&

TENCENT

THE STORY OF AN ONLINE CHINESE EMPIRE

Published by
LID Publishing Limited
The Record Hall, Studio 204,
16-16a Baldwins Gardens,
London EC1N 7RJ, UK

524 Broadway, 11th Floor, Suite 08-120,
New York, NY 10012, US

info@lidpublishing.com
www.lidpublishing.com

A member of:

www.businesspublishersroundtable.com

Published in collaboration with the China Translation & Publishing House
(a member of the China Publishing Group Corporation)

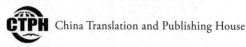 China Translation and Publishing House

© LID Publishing Limited, 2017
© China Translation and Publishing House, 2017
Reprinted in 2018

Printed in Great Britain by TJ International
ISBN: 978-1-911498-28-5

Illustration: Myriam El Jerari
Cover and Page design: Caroline Li

MA HUATENG & TENCENT

THE STORY OF AN ONLINE CHINESE EMPIRE

BY **LENG HU**

LONDON   MONTERREY
MADRID   SHANGHAI
MEXICO CITY   BOGOTA
NEW YORK   BUENOS AIRES
BARCELONA   SAN FRANCISCO

CONTENTS

FOREWORD

What is this thing called the internet? More importantly, what can it do for us, this modern invention that provides simple ease of access to a world of complex information. The internet represents a technological and cultural revolution, which has heralded a new era of industrial development – all at the click of a button.

In terms of Tencent QQ – popularly known as QQ – its founder, Pony Ma, captured the internet's most revolutionary aspect: communication. QQ has become an indispensable part of people's lives as communication has moved from traditional mediums, such as the telephone and letters, to networked communication. With QQ's little penguin logo and mascot, Pony Ma created a miracle inside the Chinese internet's 'experience economy'. He has allowed countless netizens to discover the ease and magic of online exchange at the touch of their fingertips.

Certainly, Pony Ma is one of the earliest classic examples of an internet enthusiast, as well as representative of the new economic age in China. His fortune happily coincided with a period of reform and openness in the People's Republic of China that bestowed a new atmosphere of creativity and provided a solid grounding in technology. This helped turn many entrepreneurs' dreams into reality. In a sense, the internet age in China represents a new kind of individualism and an emphasis upon the individual pursuit of dreams and aspirations.

No doubt the QQ kingdom Pony Ma created greatly changed people's notions of social interaction and helped to reshape ideas regarding interpersonal connection. It allowed people to reveal themselves through a new virtual world as they interacted with others. It made the conventional way of socialising more efficient and cheaper. It was a small piece of software that could link the entire world.

As communication has moved online, the evolution of exchange has taken on new forms. Tencent and netizens are not the only beneficiaries of this development. The whole internet age has benefited. Communication, through apps like QQ, has lubricated the gears of revolution and has led people towards a more advanced age.

CHAPTER

1

AN ENGINEER
WITH COMMERCIAL
ACUMEN

UNSUITED TO ASTRONOMY

Born in Shantou in Guangdong and brought up in Hainan, Pony Ma gained his sense of limitless wonder for the unknown world from the bright starry skies of his childhood.

His fascination with those starry skies resulted in a desperate longing for an astronomer's telescope. At first, his family was unresponsive; even Ma himself knew his request was excessive. Nevertheless, he felt obliged to vent in his diary: "My parents' approach could kill the astronomer within me." Later, his mother, on accidentally seeing his diary, began putting aside money for him to buy him the much-coveted telescope.

From the moment he received the instrument, Pony Ma would gaze transfixed towards the heavens. Years later people would ask him: "What would you say is the proudest moment in your life?" Earnestly, he would reply that it was photographing Halley's Comet in 1986 for a small cash prize.

His father, Ma Chenshu, was a cadre and former accountant for the Hainan Port Authority. His highest position in life had been as board member of a listed Shenzhen company. In addition, he shared a hometown with Hong Kong businessman Li Ka-shing, one of the richest men in the world. Li provided venture capital to Tencent, and so everyone knew his father's network had provided Pony Ma with not inconsiderable power. Ma Chenshu also acted as the accountant for Tencent when it was newly established, and provided his son with both direct and indirect instruction.

It was not just Ma Chenshu who helped Pony Ma, though. His mother, Huang Huiqing, was a prime example of the strong woman in the old adage of the 'woman behind every successful man': for a long time she occupied the post of Tencent's legal representative. Pony Ma once claimed that this was because, at the time, the legal representative of a newly launched company had to be a retiree or unemployed, and so he utilised her help.

But we digress.

In 1984, a 13-year-old Pony Ma followed his parents to live in Shenzhen, attending the best middle school there. In an environment where the motto of, 'time is money, efficiency is life' ruled, a work ethic was gradually nurtured in the young boy. His personality and ways of thinking were not yet set, but they would grow alongside that of Shenzhen, China's most youthful city. Perhaps he felt himself inseparable from the city at this point, choosing to take his final *gaokao* examinations at nearby Shenzhen University.

It might be expected that someone as obsessed with astronomy as Pony Ma might have taken astronomy as a major. But his studies had refined his ideals. As he gazed into the heavens, he realized astronomy was far removed from everyday reality, and so chose his other love, computing, as his major, perhaps seeing some commonality between the unknown universe and the potential for new discoveries in the developing field of computing. Indeed, computing and astronomy shared some attributes: both of them attempted to explore mysterious worlds, providing Ma with an outlet for his natural curiosities and skills.

In his fourth year at Shenzhen University, he was already an outstanding talent in computing. But his graduating thesis was unexpectedly practical: an analysis of the stock market. With this outstanding piece of work he graduated with ease and received his Bachelor's Degree.

An internet company, aware of his work, showed interest in purchasing one of his programs, and gave him the remarkable sum of ¥50,000, a huge amount for the time.

In spite of such initial success, Ma remained modest and, after calm consideration, decided to take up employment in order to continue accruing valuable experience before making any further decisions.

His patience and modesty, in combination with his steadiness and calm, allowed him to navigate this first junction in the road and to take advantage of the situation, with an eye to potential future benefits. If we carefully examine how Ma planned his life, we can see a steady and sure enterprise: he always had his feet planted firmly on the ground and began from practical realities, providing a firm foundation for a bright but uncertain future.

TAKING OFF

In 1993, Ma graduated. He went to Runxun Communications Development Company as a software engineer. Runxun was established in 1990, its main operations involving paging services. Relying on the concept that the market should determine services, the company created a number of famous products. Runxun's red advertising banner – *One Call, Connecting China* – was a recognizable symbol all over the streets of China.

Between 1995 and 1998, the company's legendary status reached its uppermost heights. Although Ma was not a well-known figure in the company, he rode its fortunes and saw his vision gradually widen and expand, as he refined his ability to explore problems from different perspectives and vantages.

There were two distinct skill sets in which Runxun particularly assisted Ma. One such area was that of instruction in management skills. He learned how to construct and govern a large-scale company, and how to compete and aquire a share in a new market. He also learned how to gain capital from Hong Kong, Runxun having been listed on Hong Kong's stock exchange.

Secondly, he had access to some of Runxun's earliest clients and customers. As he was forming Tencent, he worked on the launch of a complete service for pager customers at Runxun. Working at the most famous telecommunication company in the country allowed him to make many connections in the industry. These connections gave Tencent an edge over the competition.

In Runxun, he learned a completely new approach to the development of software. Its great significance lay not in creating dazzling programs, but functional and efficient ones. As a result, he was interested not in manufacturing the most creative designs, but the most practical, which would be used by the greatest number of people.

Day after day, faced with all variety of projects, he would work, unwearied. His fascination with computers grew. He further developed the knowledge he had gained during his degree, and his reputation grew along with his skills.

In the third year of his employment at Runxun, he began to engage in side interests – among them, the mighty Chinese fidonet, or CFido.

CFido came into existence in 1991, and was most popular between 1993 and 1998. It was a BBS internet network, linked by telephone wire and based on peer-to-peer sharing. Computer enthusiasts (or 'geeks') independently created and maintained the system in their spare time.

As a veteran geek, Ma took a great interest in CFido. After half a year testing the program, he decided to set up a substation in Shenzhen. In 1995, using four telephone lines, he connected eight computers and set up his Shenzhen branch, calling it Ponysoft – the "Pony" coming from the English translation of his last name.

Taking care of Ponysoft on the one hand and working at Runxun on the other, his attention began gradually to shift towards the former – not least because CFido was attracting more high-end talent, from whom he could learn about the frontiers of programming.

Working patiently in seclusion until he could realize his potential was one of the secrets to Ma's success, and something many others were unable to do. He had an instinct for when to attack and when to withdraw. Through using his knowledge of himself and his environment, he was able to lessen the probability of any negative or ill-judged decisions.

Once, in an interview with Shanghai's *Waitan Magazine*, he explained that he was a capital market entrepreneur as well as a software engineer, yet had always preferred the latter side and retained an inexhaustible interest in programming. As Tencent's product range grew, he would occasionally assume the role of the company's chief product tester – not only testing the products personally, but those of other companies as well. Once, he even proudly stated that he had tested every piece of instant messaging software the company had released.

One day, while surfing the internet, he happened to come across a messaging app called ICQ. In an instant, his attention was captured. The discovery would prove a major turning point in his life.

Instant messaging provides many wonderful benefits, but what precisely is it? From a technological point of view, it is a form of communication software that has consistently proven to be superior to the alternative electronic means of communication. It combines the immediacy of the telephone with the simultaneity of email in an effective hybrid form.

Before instant messaging became commonplace, the range of functional possibilities it offered seemed unimaginable. This was because, along with the ceaseless reinvention and perfection of instant messaging technology, it was able to move offline into the spheres of voice messaging, email, net conferencing and SMS – a complete one-stop shop. In addition to these benefits, this compilation of functions could be organized, easily assimilated and learned by users.

Instant messaging was created by three young men from Israel. Initially, they had simply planned to create a communication tool for their own use, but their insight destined the small program for greatness. Eventually it became a widely-used online communication tool. Yet, in the beginning, it was simply a way to communicate between three people.

The three Jewish men proudly dubbed their software 'I seek you'. For convenience, this became simply 'ICQ'. As they became more adept at writing the program, they formed a company called Mirabilis, which officially launched ICQ to the public. At its largest, the share price and development of Mirabilis attracted much attention, allowing the company to be sold to America Online (AOL), one of the world's largest websites, for US$287 million.

After entering the market, ICQ gained a popular following among a large number of netizens, soon becoming an integral and essential part of people's daily life online.

ICQ's considerable power can be seen in how it was able gain precedence in the world of the internet in such a short period of time. However there were setbacks and weaknesses that prevented ICQ sustaining its development in China. In a world of competing internet heroes, those who take the lead often have a considerable advantage. However, ICQ lost its best chance to take advantage of this principle in China due to three crucial factors: firstly, there was the problem of business philosophy. The founders of ICQ were not fully aware that their arrival heralded a major revolution in communication technology, and so they failed to make plans to promote the product globally.

In addition, their market was restricted to English-language users. To make matters worse, even after ICQ became widely utilised, management were unable to adjust their marketing tactics, continuing to stick with conventional approaches. Opportunities were missed and their competitors overtook them.

The second factor to hinder the potential of ICQ was the operating environment. To survive in a global communication network, instant messaging must transcend geographical limits and network communication tools. Issues of software compatibility, user habits and other factors doomed ICQ's attempts to successfully transplant the software to a foreign country. They failed to take positive measures to rectify the fact that ICQ users and non-users were unable to overcome the communication barriers between ICQ's software, a factor that greatly restricted ICQ's expansion. While the US internet had combined the software of AOL Instant Messenger and ICQ to produce a simple, functional version called ICQLite, it was difficult to replicate the same success in China.

The final problem was presented by the language barrier. This was ICQ's fatal flaw – not having native language availability. Since it was introduced in English, it was always difficult for those from non-English speaking countries to use. The only users in China who were not restricted by this language barrier were those with English-speaking ability.

Although ICQ did not go far in the Chinese market, without a doubt it opened the world of instant messaging, allowing people to realize the possibilities of a technology that could connect people across great distances.

The greatest benefactor of ICQ's influence on China was Ma. As a veteran computer enthusiast and internet user, early access to ICQ captured his attention. He would often communicate online through ICQ with friends, wandering through the wondrous avenues of communication and discovery opened by the internet age.

After some time using ICQ, it occurred to Ma that there were a billion people in China and, given the great demand for instant messaging software, the Chinese needed their own native instant messaging software.

Ma considered not only how to develop his own software, but how to make it bigger and better than ICQ. Several years of webmaster experience no longer sated his appetite; in an era when everyone was battling for internet supremacy, he wanted to devote more time and energy to launching his own entrepreneurial career.

SPARING NO EFFORT

In April 2010, in an interview with *Chinese Entrepreneurs*, Ma said: "When I first began thinking about what the internet can bring, I was involved in pager technology, and my first thought was how the internet could be made to function like a pager. I wondered how to combine the two technologies' operating systems, in order to bring something to the paging industry and forestall its decline. Because I could see that it was a sunset industry, from the moment mobile phones were arriving and text messaging was becoming popular."

Not only did Runxun lack strategic vision, the whole paging industry was blind to their bleak prospects. Their moment in the sun created a collective blindness and, from 2000, when a turning point in the market arrived, virtually all paging companies spiralled into panic. By 2001 they were facing the end, and, in 2002, complete extinction. Ultimately, the once-bright Runxun sacrificed some of their customers to a large telecom company called Liantong.

In addition to the decline of the paging industry, there was also an external factor that affected Ma's plans for the future. Ding Lei, the founder of NetEase, took seven months to write his free-to-use Wangyi email software and sold it for ¥1.19 million to Guangzhou's Feihua network. Ma felt acutely conscious that the internet was a goldmine of opportunities that was simply lying there, waiting. With opportunities passing him by, he could not afford to remain on the sidelines any longer.

Ma's business idea was simply to explore new paths on the internet, in order to find how he might add value. There was a rumour suggesting that Ma had asked Runxun about the possibility of developing a piece of software like QQ, but that this forward-thinking proposal had failed to catch the attention of management, who were unable to realize the development potential of such a small piece of software.

The reason management had trouble recognizing its potential was that they failed to recognize the importance of customer information, preferring, instead, to focus purely on profit. In reality, customer loyalty, not wealth, may be said to be the most important resource in business; perhaps for this reason, Ma recognized that his approach was not compatible with Runxun's and that he would be better served by focusing on his own business.

In October 1998, China's internet entered a period of rapid development. In that year, Charles Zhang founded Sohu, and Zhou Hongyi created 3721: two companies that excited the IT community and created a flurry of activity. Others quickly launched businesses, hoping to carve a place for themselves on this new battlefield.

Ma, of course, was no exception. Although he did not yet have a clear idea of the specific area of focus upon which to direct his business, his course was already determined: combining paging technology with the internet. His reason for settling on such a goal was that he already had five years of professional experience in these areas, and this accumulated capital could help him.

But he couldn't do it alone; he would need to find a team. His first comrade was Zhang Zhidong, a fellow computer studies student from Shenzhen University. After graduation Zhang had gone to South China University of Technology to major in computing, gaining a Master's degree. He then returned to Shenzhen to work on the technical team of Shenzhen-Shanghai stock trading software at an increasingly famous computer company.

When he and Ma were studying in Shenzhen University they were both top students, but Zhang was the top of the top – even compared to all the other computer experts in Shenzhen.

One month after Ma and Zhang established Tencent, the company's third founder entered the scene: Zeng Liqing. Zeng was a communications student from Xidian University. After graduation he had gained a stable job at Shenzhen Telecom. At that time, Ma and Zhang had been classmates from middle school to university, along with the daughter of the President of the Shenzhen Computing Association. Zeng met Ma and Zhang when they were invited to one of the association's activities.

Zeng had the boldness and courage of a pioneer, and Shenzhen was one of the first areas to push forward broadband. The project had nearly failed, but Zeng relied on his efforts to see it through to success – the same effort he would bring to the futures market, which was quite an achievement in the 1990s.

Besides these three, Tencent's other two founders were Xu Chenye and Chen Yidan. Xu Chenye was also a classmate of Ma and Zhang in Shenzhen University's computing department. He later studied computer science at Nanjing University as a graduate student, before working for Shenzhen's telecom branch along with Zeng Liqing. Easygoing of character, Xu Chenye was known as something of a 'Mr Nice Guy'.

Chen Yidan, formerly known as Chen Yizhou, had been a classmate of Ma's at Shenzhen middle school, and a chemistry major at Shenzhen University. He had changed his name because of the fame of another Chen Yizhou, who was renowned as the CEO and founder of the company ChinaRen. Chen was a scrupulous lawyer, and knew how to arouse enthusiasm in those around him.

Four brothers, then, and comrades in Ma's enterprise – now it was time to realize his ambitions for expansion.

CHAPTER

ENTREPRENEURSHIP IS NOT A GAME OF MAHJONG

KEEP YOUR EYES ON ANY SETBACKS, AND MOVE FORWARD

In November 1998, Pony Ma and Zheng Zhidong jointly registered Shenzhen Tencent Computer Systems Ltd. They called the company Tencent owing to links with Ma's own name, and various influences on his career: Pony Ma's name contained a character pronounced something like "Ten", meaning to soar upward. The "cent" character was due to the influence of his former company, Runxun, as the "xun" sound, changed to a vaguely similar English equivalent, became "cent".

Each founding member assumed a Tencent QQ number: 10001 to 10005. In order to carry out their duties, they were all allotted a separate 'sphere of influence': Pony Ma and Chen Yidan were CEOs; Zhang Zhidong was chief technology officer; Xu Chenye was chief information officer; and Zeng Liqing was chief operating officer.

In terms of their respective share investments, Pony Ma held 47.5%, Zheng Zhidong 20%, Zeng Liqing 12.5%, and Chen Yidan and Xu Chenye each held 10%. Although Ma had originally the greatest stake, he had arranged for his proportion of shares to be dropped to less than half, in order to prevent a monopolistic, dictatorial situation. At the same time, Ma insisted that he be responsible for the company's primary funds, because he didn't want the equity to be too dispersed and did not wish for any single person to have the ultimate decision regarding any crucial questions.

In the company's early days, Pony Ma and his team struggled: they were bewildered at times by the problem of finding their future direction, and they were struck with regret when the day-to-day work of the company met many challenges.

Despite these initial struggles, their venture was an unmitigated success: by their tenth year, in 2008, the seemingly small and potentially insignificant company had accumulated a set of statistics that could only be described as awe-inspiring. QQ's total number of users had reached 856.2 million, with active users at 355.1 million; they had a record of 45.3 million simultaneous online users; monthly payments from users for value-added services of 30.3 million; and mobile and telecommunications value-added services paid monthly by 14.8 million users. Tencent's third quarter income was up to ¥2.245 billion – half a billion more than the aggregate income of Baidu and Alibaba during the same period. Alibaba and Baidu were China's second and third biggest internet companies respectively.

Tencent's start-up capital was ¥500,000, at that time by no means a small sum of money. But for fairly small internet companies, if strong and robust investors cannot be found, and profitability cannot be found, no matter how much initial funding may exist, it will eventually be exhausted.

Ma did not fashion himself as an unchallengeable tycoon, but simply as someone trying to bring the worlds of internet and pagers more closely together, in order to create a kind of wireless paging system. Tencent's main clients at the outset were Shenzhen Telecom, Unicom and some paging stations in Shenzhen. Pony Ma was most interested in the development of instant messaging software; this was a tangential project he was developing.

This only existed as a side project initially, for similar reasons as to those which had motivated Runxun management's rejection of Pony Ma's proposals: people could not see any immediate profit in the messaging software. Of course, Pony Ma knew the development potential, but at the outset of Tencent, it was financially impossible to invest capital in the project.

The founders of the company faced many challenges in the initial phases of starting up: they did not initially understand marketing, or how to effectively move their products; they would attempt to market them to telecommunications operators, but often found the door slammed in their face.

Tencent's five founders avoided being crushed by the dangers that followed the opening of the market. After their failures, they would actively encourage each other; after every attempt, they would always find users willing to accept them. Ultimately, this persistence and positive attitude of mutual encouragement paid off.

On 11 February 1999, Tencent finally developed a Chinese software for ICQ: QICQ. It was officially launched online, becoming the key that would lift Tencent to new heights.

The gap between QICQ and the QQ of today was immeasurably big, and QICQ was indeed just a Chinese version of ICQ with no special qualities of its own. It earned Tencent the accusation from many that they were simply a copycat company.

However, let us consider the situation at the time: Tencent had just ten employees, and only a few million yuan in funds. Yet they also wanted to conduct their own independent research and software development, limited though they were by funds and technological capability. There was little choice but to pursue a policy of 'research by mimicry'.

Pony Ma's next step was to find a solution for making the QICQ software profitable, and so they began looking for a suitable buyer. At that time, some of the country's banking and post offices were able to provide 10 or 20 million yuan to finance projects by internet companies like Tencent. Pony Ma, who was actively engaging with a number of companies and organizations, promoted QICQ to them, seeking over ¥300,000. Unfortunately, Pony Ma's bid failed, losing out to a Guangzhou telecommunications company.

Although the failed bid seemed a crushing blow at the time, in retrospect, it was beneficial for the company. If their bid had succeeded, the QICQ patent would have fallen into the hands of others and thus slipped from their grasp. In Ma's view, the difficulties and pressures they faced were only temporary. As long as they kept focused on the present, good fortune would come.

The 'emperor penguin' would prove to be the very thing that heralded QICQ's rising fortunes.

In copying ICQ, Pony Ma and his associates had discovered areas where the program was lacking. For example, all of a user's information was saved in the area where they logged in; once a user changed computers, the contacts they had added and all their information were lost. In addition, ICQ only allowed users to chat with friends who were also online, and required the information provided by users in order to help them search for friends. It had a weak search capability, and the user experience left a great deal of room for improvement.

These seemingly subtle differences, and the scope to improve upon the challenges they presented for users, were capable of placing a company at a great advantage on the Chinese internet. Many netizens in China were surfing through internet bars, and naturally they would wish to have their QICQ information stored in the server and not the client profile or individual computer. Ma recognized that ICQ's vulnerabilities and weaknesses provided opportunities for improvement. He prepared a program that allowed users, no matter how many times they changed computer, to retain the friends they had added.

Meanwhile, he attempted to meet users' needs by allowing them to message offline users and to chat with anyone else who was online. QICQ also allowed users to select a personalized avatar. MSN launched a similar function a few years later, proving to the world the value of the improvements Pony Ma had made.

A new challenge now presented itself: how to allow more potential users to understand and use QICQ. There was only one way: publicity.

Ma knew that a modern business required clever marketing. Among those large Chinese web portals that had received foreign investment, all had, without exception, engaged in massive marketing campaigns that left people in awe.

Tencent had yet to receive any venture capital. Pondering over the reasons behind this, Ma had no choice but to carve another path. He promoted the company through BBS forums, personally visiting online the BBS forums of domestic universities to put up his advertisements.

The plan worked, proving his sharp tactical vision. Owing to the fact that the spread of the internet in China happened relatively late, those who were familiar with it were predominantly young and based in universities. They had an appetite for the internet and a love of being online and understanding the technology. Aiming advertising at them proved an effective and purposeful method of satisfying a growing, and hungry, market. Soon, many university students were QICQ users.

Ma's other marketing tactic lay in internet cafes. Due to the fact that home computers were relatively rare, people would go to internet cafes to get online. These cafes all had a number of pre-installed programs; thus, advertising QICQ through them seemed to provide one of the most efficient means of gaining publicity.

Not long after, Pony Ma's 'Penguin Age' arrived: in November 1999, the number of QICQ users soared to 1 million, reaching 5 million in April 2000. On 9 May 2001, the number of US users of ICQ broke the 100 million mark, eliminating any doubts about the potential of online messaging and confirming the wisdom of AOL's decision to buy ICQ for US$287 million in 1998. However, the Americans' engagement with online messaging was matched by the growth in China – by the end of 2001, China's number of QICQ users had exceeded 90 million. Even more surprisingly, QICQ's users were growing at the speed of nearly 390,000 every day.

Matching or surpassing the growth of ICQ was just a matter of time. The number of QICQ users had grown from 0 to 90 million in a period of three years. An examination of the figures might seem to suggest that the growth was effortless. However, behind the scenes, Pony Ma and his team were constantly honing and testing their product. With the rapid rise of QICQ, ICQ finally discovered the presence of this silently growing 'twin brother', and were suspicious of its sources and legitimacy. A technology patent lawsuit was inevitable.

As QICQ became increasingly popular, ICQ grew nervous. Between August and September 1999, Tencent received two letters online from the US, stating that they had patented the letters ICQ, and that when Tencent registered, on 26 January 1999, the domain name oicq.com, and, on 7 November 1998, oicq.net, they violated intellectual property rights. AOL were requesting Tencent transfer, free of charge, both domain names to them.

Ma did not provide a clear response to either request. But AOL appeared to be serious, and on 3 March 2000, they officially submitted their case to the National Arbitration Forum in Minnesota, as well as submitting the details of their arbitration case to Tencent.

3

CHAPTER

THE WOLF OF THE CAPITAL WORLD

By November 1999, QQ's user numbers had increased to 1 million. For Ma, the news was a source of both excitement and anxiety: on the one hand, they could claim a growing number of users; on the other, the financial pressure upon the company was also growing. In the second half of 1999, Ma held discussions with the other founders and they collectively decided to sell part of their stake, as this would allow them to utilise a large proportion of QQ's users as a bargaining chip.

Ma later recalled the incident: "In 1998, when I first founded Tencent, the internet industry in China was just beginning. At that time there were only 3 million internet users, a fraction of the more than 300 million that currently exist – 100 times more! The environment was not so good at that time. Access to venture capital had just begun, and opportunities were few."

At first Ma considered finding a bank. But he discovered that the gap between the banks and the emerging internet industry remained a large one. They did not have the slightest interest in QQ's users, because they could not see the possibility that, one day in the future, there might be money to be made from the little penguin's non-fee-paying users.

Ma was worried. He knew he would have to find some other way of sustaining and nurturing his fledgling business; he would have to find another route. Later, he discovered that opportunities for financing from overseas were far more plentiful, and changed his original plan to seek foreign investment.

In accordance with the provisions Tencent had defined at its outset, Ma was solely responsible for the financing. However, the lack of money had become such a pressing issue that, in addition to Ma, another CEO, Zeng Liqing, was enlisted to help.

At that time Tencent was valued at US$5.5 million, and Zeng hoped to raise US$2.2 million, which would yield about 40% of shares. US$2.2 million was the figure the five founders had agreed upon, with 40% representing the value they could withstand – their bottom line.

In order to attract foreign investment, Ma planned meticulously, afraid of appearing vulnerable. The crux of his proposal was that Tencent required money to buy servers and increase its bandwidth. However, the plan was less specific regarding how they would make a profit, referring mostly to membership fees and advertising. In fact, membership fees and advertising were common to most internet companies, and it was difficult to highlight any features or advantages unique to Tencent. The plan did not mention proposals for text messaging charges, anime and value added services, and (perhaps the most profitable opportunity) online gaming. All the potential highlights of the plan were therefore obscured.

Although Zeng Liqing has become one of China's most appealing angel investors, at this point in time, when financing was still relatively new, there were few convenient financing channels. Zeng's plan was simple: find a few acquaintances who could make recommendations.

The first person occurring to Zeng was Alvin Liu, with whom he and several of Tencent's founders had a good personal relationship. In addition there was Zhang Zhidong, a former colleague. Both had worked at emerging computer companies. During Tencent's earlier 1 million capital increase and share expansion, Zeng had borrowed money from Alvin Liu.

Alvin Liu offered to help introduce Zeng to investors. Zeng in turn promised 5% of any finance secured to Alvin. Alvin recommended Tencent to IDG (Pacific Risk Technology Funds). Zeng, for his part, identified Hong Kong's Pacific Century Cyberworks as a potential source of finance.

IDG and Pacific Century Cyberworks both wanted to make investments in Tencent. Not because of the commercial plan of some 20 pages prepared by Ma and his team, but because of the story about how ICQ had been sold to America Online for US$287 million. Perhaps both companies felt that QQ was the Chinese version of ICQ – not worth hundreds of millions of US dollars, so much as millions. Indeed, if ICQ could find popularity across the globe, then why was QQ in China not booming?

Thus, in the first half of 2000, after the first phase of financing in Tencent, the founding employees held 60% of the shares, while IDG and Pacific Century CyberWorks of Hong Kong took US$1.1 million worth of shares at 20% each.

US$2.2 million for an internet venture seemed a comparatively small sum of money, particularly when many companies received multiple millions. However the money was crucial to the company's advancement: with the investment, many of Ma's ideas would soon become a reality. He used the money to improve the hardware facilities. They bought up servers and bandwidth – 200,000 IBM servers. They also strengthened the development and improvement of QQ's software. Not long after this point, QQ had overtaken the competition and become a leader. The arrival of QQ's new devices filled Ma with endless satisfaction.

Many entrepreneurs experience hardship, and Ma was no exception. After receiving financial assistance, he began to concentrate on continuing to innovate his Instant Messaging programs. He believed that, although many people could not see the grand potential of QQ, it was only a matter of time before all these possibilities would be realized.

THE GENTLEST PHILOSOPHY OF FINANCING IN HISTORY

After the first round, Ma and his team were working hard on their various advancements, while the investors observed from the sidelines having noted that there had been no changes apart from Tencent's purchase of a few servers. Even when Ma again found himself financially stretched and looking for investors, they were no longer willing, thinking that the little penguin should have been satiated. More money would have felt like throwing away their equity share, and so they refused to lend a penny to Tencent.

At that time, IDG was more positive, and helped to find buyers to support the company through the crisis. In contrast, Pacific Century's attitude was unclear. There had been a time when they said they would consider providing more money, but later they seemed hesitant, and Ma could neither fathom their thoughts, nor predict their final decision. Eventually they met Richard Li, a major Hong Kong businessman, at a tea garden restaurant and signed an investment agreement with Pacific Century, who provided a fairly generous deposit.

Pacific Century also recommended the company to its associated business, the TOM group. Although TOM group had high-level exchanges with Tencent, they could not agree to invest. With the investment of over US$1 million, the rejection did not prevent IDG and Pacific Century from doing their best to help Ma afterward.

What Ma did not expect was that, as he and the team worked feverishly for the little penguin, they would encounter the 'internet winter'.

Just when Ma was worrying about the source of their next round of financing, an American appeared at Tencent's office. He was from Milad International Holding Group (MIH) and held the position of Vice President of China operations for the company.

MIH was no ordinary investor, and had more than simply deep pockets and ambition. Their main business was interactive television and pay TV, and at that time they had reached an annual turnover of tens of millions and a market value of more than US$4 billion. They were greatly interested in China's internet companies and were looking for a reliable partner with whom to enter the Chinese market.

MIH's Vice President had a wide range of investments and helped MIH form ties with Tencent. In 2001, MIH bought a 20% stake in Tencent from Pacific Century and a 13% stake from IDG. But MIH realized they had been overly timid when they saw Tencent's development. They did not want to merely play the role of a supporting equity investor.

In June 2002, changes were made to Tencent's ownership structure. After careful consultation with MIH, it was decided that the specific management of Tencent was up to Ma and the others. MIH would be restricted to two non-executive directors, who would not have specific regulatory powers.

In this regard, Ma's position was very clear: he could not let outsiders gain control. To do so would be worse than never having gained external financial investment in the first place.

Ma's insistence on such a management structure avoided the potential for much conflict, and reflected his vision as a strategic manager. Of course, MIH also brought stability to Tencent's shareholding structure – another important factor in Tencent's success.

At this crucial point, Ma had pulled through and avoided a crisis, as well as having gained valuable experience as part of the process. Maturing while simultaneously making a profit: perhaps this was the only option available to an entrepreneurial enterprise, and for its leader.

MAKING REAL PROGRESS

In the spring of 2000, QQ recorded 100,000 simultaneous users, and Ma sent out an enthusiastic press release. Not long afterwards, to Ma's great excitement, the *People's Daily* reprinted the article online.

Until August 2001, Ma felt satisfied and tranquil regarding finances, the business having found a new source of income. Tencent and Guangdong Mobile signed a cooperation agreement, which would allow QQ users to talk in real time with any mobile user in Guangdong who had both QQ and SMS. In the new age of communication, this was a herald of the dawn of a new age for netizens.

Through its smooth progress in cooperating with Guangdong Mobile, Tencent achieved profitability, and, thanks to advancements in internet messaging technology, it soon held half of the market's share in text messaging.

In the wake of Tencent's business improvement, Ma found other tools to make money apart from SMS, including advertising, QQ's mobile service, and the fees of QQ's member businesses. Among these, the greatest source of profit was the outsourcing of QQ's brand, from which Ma made a 10% agency fee.

Seeing the little penguin's fortunes escalate, Ma realized that those areas that many people wrote off as unprofitable could turn out to be anything but. With great passion, he would say that they had not realized how to use QQ's money until the company from Guangzhou had come calling, showing great sincerity and, to Ma's great surprise, providing hundreds of thousands of dollars.

Although this achievement was inseparable from Ma's own efforts, the evolution of the internet and changes in its environment also played a role. Ma's idea at the time was that earning money would help to promote Tencent, effectively killing two birds with one stone.

Not long afterwards QQ began to launch news broadcasts, informing people where to buy toys. This simple communication became emblematic, and spread to other forms, like online dating and online friendships. From this point onwards, QQ became a cultural symbol, not simply a piece of instant messaging software. In this growing culture, new words like "online relationship" and "online friends" began to appear.

In August 2000, QQ introduced banner advertising. According to statistics from December of the same year, Tencent's revenue from advertising had reached ¥1.5 million. The bursting of the internet bubble had little effect on QQ. At its worst, advertising revenue had halved by February 2001; but by March it had picked up again.

Apart from traditional means of profit, such as advertising, Tencent introduced paid memberships. Tencent had over 3,000 members, each of whom contributed between ¥120 and ¥200 a year. Although their numbers were few compared to those of ordinary users, they were at the vanguard of new profit-making initiatives at Tencent.

By the end of 2001, Tencent had successfully achieved a net profit of ¥10.22 million. In 2002, this increased to ¥144 million – more than ten times the previous year. By 2003, when it stood at ¥338 million, profit had nearly doubled compared to 2002's figures.

By 2004, Tencent would achieve a record ¥1.144 billion turnover, a 55% increase. They had also achieved net profits of ¥446 million – a 38% increase.

From this point on, Ma finally began to enjoy a sense of stability and achievement. He was transitioning from being a struggling entrepreneur to a figure emblematic of accomplishment, and he was beginning to draw attention. People were becoming conscious of his acumen and started to herald him as a success. However, only a few understood the determination, hard work and struggle that lay behind the shining façade of his achievements.

THE BIG BREAK

During the early days of his startup, Ma had always actively searched for new ways to make money for the little penguin, welcoming anybody, so long as they could earn profit and would not hurt the core of QQ's identity. His view in this respect was becoming increasingly diverse, as he discovered new opportunities in many areas.

At the end of 2000, China Mobile officially introduced the majority of its users to something called 'Monternet'. No one could have guessed at the way in which this new value chain would save a large number of internet companies – and that Ma would be one of the major benefactors.

The situation Ma was facing was that of hundreds of millions of registered internet users, and a great deal of consumer demand. Unfortunately, Ma could find no means of levying a fee, and Monternet's phone charge suddenly reminded Ma that there was an acceptable means to impose a fee.

Soon, Tencent launched a mobile service for QQ. It wasn't long before QQ mobile became the backbone of Monternet, its shares at their highest point representing 70%.

In 2002 and 2003, two new QQ services were launched, offering SMS, ring tones and online dating services. Ma also created online games for a university.

Similar to online gaming, the purpose of Ma's information portal had an overriding purpose – to open up the market for online advertising. Advertisers wanted to gain access to influential websites, and gateway websites were the easiest place to build influence. Although Ma felt the size of the market was larger than that for online advertising, the potential for growth for advertising was larger than that for games, and so it would be worthwhile developing an online portal.

However, there was a problem: many users had become accustomed to QQ's emphasis on youth interests and entertainment. To break this link would require the addition of more sophisticated portals, and a new name and identity. Ma also took into account the need to have a clear division between the brands of the portals and chat tools.

His solution was that, when it became clear that the users would no longer need entertainment, they would drop it of their own accord. He did not want any negative feedback from users.

Soon, 'Tencent Net' was born. In order to transform it into a high-end brand, Ma recruited new staff on a large scale. He also agreed to sponsor the 2010 Shanghai World Expo, a golden opportunity to build up the portal's image.

Under the agreement, Tencent was responsible for creating an online platform for the Expo, in addition to its interactive and e-commerce platforms. Ma indicated that the exposure would mean that more people would recognize and acknowledge that Tencent was not simply a chat tool.

Under Ma's strategic planning, Tencent's portal website and online gaming were a success. The next plan was to test the water in the area of value-added services.

In fact, although the concept of value-added services was not clear to many users, had they been asked what 'Q coins' were, they would have been very aware. For Ma, these seemingly insignificant gimmicks and the rapid growth of online gaming could ensure the proper functioning and development of the company, while simultaneously providing opportunities for Tencent's portal and e-commerce outlets.

In 2001, Tencent officially released a ¥120-a-year Q card. Not long after this, a paid version of QQ and a chess-themed game followed. This paid version of QQ had virtual game-like properties and allowed users to choose virtual clothing.

It is said that when the new version of QQ was approved, the 80-page proposal led to serious and probing discussions with What is PPT?, despite Tencent's relative lack in confidence in the new venture at the time. It had, however, since become the most profitable part of Tencent, and made Ma a much-lauded hero in the world of value-added services.

Ma had a subtle and distinct business philosophy, which others had dubbed the 'Three Self-Questions'. He was said to have frequently asked himself the following three questions in situations where the wisdom of engaging in a new business initiative had to be assessed:

Question 1: Can you be an expert in a new area?

A competitor might be interested in business, profits, and capital, but not necessarily take customer demand into account. In contrast, Ma possessed what might have appeared, to the internet market, to be a vague sense of understanding regarding the technicalities of the particular business area in question, but was actually a sharp instinct, which helped Tencent to achieve direction. He possessed a kind of frenzied interest and enthusiasm with which to build Tencent's framework, which placed technology at its core. This concept in particular was at the heart of the company's daily production and business: a focus on technology development and quality improvement.

Question 2: If you don't do it, who will?

The real value of developing software lay in its practicality to the user, rather than in the happiness it brought to the developer. Ma said: "I'm just someone who really loves the internet, and what those who use it most need, what will be most useful for us to have – that's all."

Question 3: Once completed, can the new project maintain a competitive advantage?

In the second half of 1999, when the paging market was growing, Ma faced a crucial choice: on the one hand, the paging market had shown a decline; on the other, QQ's users had increased to 1 million and the number was steadily growing. Ma was still not aware of QQ's potential. Whether in technology or capital, he lacked confidence in grasping QQ's competitive advantage. To this end, Tencent's strategy was three-pronged: firstly, focus on perfecting QQ's function and developing a new version; secondly, seek funding support from investors; thirdly and finally, continue to strengthen the technology of traditional pagers.

Later, many people would see that Ma's path had been correct. In fact, it was not Ma who contributed to Tencent, but Tencent itself that contributed a miracle.

TENCENT'S SUCCESSFUL LISTING ON THE STOCK MARKET

From 2001 to 2003, Tencent's scale and profits both grew massively. In August 2003, Tencent bought out the stake remaining in IDG and recovered a small stake from MIH after the readjustment of their ownership structure. In the end, they stood as they had before the IPO, with MIH holding a 50% stake.

Tencent's public data showed that in 2004 they enjoyed a ¥1 billion profit in the first quarter, an 87% increase over the same period in 2003. But Ma didn't want Tencent's sources of funding limited by venture capital. In order to accumulate more diversified finance channels and contribute to the stable operation of Tencent, he began plotting how to seek out and aquire other sources of finance.

Regarding the question of where to float Tencent, Ma said, "Among underwriting consultants, there were six suggesting Hong Kong, four recommending the NASDAQ, three recommending doing both...it was all making me rather big-headed. The average price-earnings ratio of Hong Kong's listed companies was low compared to the US, but I began to wonder – what if I were a market leader in Hong Kong?"

Eventually, Ma settled on Hong Kong. He explained that the stock market requirements were stricter than those of the NASDAQ. With Tencent having achieved three years of consecutive profit, they were the only Chinese internet company eligible to list in Hong Kong.

After some preparations, on 7 June 2004, Tencent, the biggest supplier of instant messaging products and the QQ service, had an IPO on the Hong Kong stock market, offering shares to overseas investors. When this was announced, there was a stir on the internet within China. Until then, few people had known Tencent was going public, as Ma had feared that too many headlines would cause a media panic.

Tencent was officially listed for trading on the Hong Kong Stock Exchange on 16 June of the same year. At HK$3.70 per share, the company had a market value of HK$6.22 billion. After the listing, Ma was a multimillionaire.

The listing once again revealed the charms of the little penguin. Tencent caught on quickly with shareholders; and although most investors reacted more rationally, Tencent's stock horse soon bolted, the result being that it was over-subscribed 146 times over.

Ma planned to use the funds accrued from Tencent's listing to inject HK$818 million into Tencent's new strategic direction, which comprised instant messaging, entertainment, and takeover targets, including e-commerce and value-added services in music. He did not rule out future acquisitions in areas such as third-party technology developers and service providers. With the remaining HK$250 million, he would expand the company's existing business.

Some analysts pointed out that, judging from 2003, even if Ma had not raised shares, their cash flow was strong enough for them to have an instant communications and entertainment business equivalent to a small or medium company. Indeed, from the first quarter of 2004, Tencent's revenue was in a state of sustained profitability. From a financial perspective, the share listing was not, it seemed, entirely for the sake of money.

There were also some investment banks who, as major shareholders, had contributed to the company's listing solely for cash purposes. Yet a closer look at Tencent's shareholder structure would reveal that MIH should have already withdrawn its investment. Why would Ma give such a large piece of meat to Hong Kong's public shareholders?

There were also some investment banks that believed that Tencent's listing had been motivated by the decision of major shareholders, who wished to cash out on their investment. However, given its meticulous observation of Tencent's shareholding structure and business, MIH should have already recovered its investment. Why then would Ma bestow such a big gift upon public investors in Hong Kong?

Although the answer is uncertain, it can be seen that Ma adhered to the local development strategies familiar to Hong wme management and structural coordination problems after its listing, the company had mostly tended towards stabilisation and regularisation. As well as having gained a wealth of experience and wisdom regarding enterprise and business development, Ma had developed better, more scientific mechanisms of management. If the company had not been listed, it would have faced many problems in the future and a potential lack of momentum.

Along with its listing, Tencent faced the problem of encouraging staff. In 2008, Ma gave an interview to the *Beijing Youth Weekly*. Speaking of Tencent's employees, he said that both the founders and shareholders were very important and that a number of elements were vital in order to attract talent: financing, the company's image, and the circulation of shares and options.

Within a few years of listing, the company was pursuing equity incentives. It issued an equity incentive plan in December 2007: shares would be purchased by an independent trustee with the cost paid by Tencent. The plan would be adopted by 13 December 2007 and would be valid for ten years. The board granted that it would limit the total number of shares in the issued share capital to 2%, and that no individual would hold more than one 1%.

On 29 August 2008, Tencent's board decided to award 184 employees a million new shares in the company as a bonus, in a move aimed at attracting and retaining talent. On 10 July 2009, Tencent's board also launched a massive equity award programme, granting shares to a total of 1,250 employees. It was no small incentive and left people amazed.

As can be seen from this equity incentive plan, Ma had taken his team of little penguins to a fresh stage of development. With new problems arriving, he had launched novel policies to address the obstacles that lay ahead, allowing the ship to sail further through the internet's rough seas.

CHAPTER

CHALLENGES AND DIFFICULTIES

STEALING ACCOUNTS

After QQ had become an essential tool for many users, a very interesting phenomenon was born, one that surrounded users like an inescapable phantom: identity theft.

Once upon a time, identity theft on QQ was a rampant phenomenon, placing many users on the offensive: hackers stole virtual property and a social circle, in a move that could wreak havoc on the the user's work and life. Even today, when identity theft is harder and more complex, the phenomenon still exists. As a result, QQ faced more and more complaints from users.

This caused problems for Ma, who, due to the size of QQ's user base and the proliferation of professional and non-professional hackers, faced obstacles in cracking down on the problem.

On 17 January 2013, after the conclusion of the fifth meeting of the People's Congress in Shenzhen, Ma, attempting to quietly leave, found himself encircled by the media. In response to questions, he stated that, in 2013, a major priority for Tencent would be improving information security.

Ma's words were not merely reassuring rhetoric: in 2013, Tencent had 20,000 employees, of whom 2,000 were specialists in information security. Tencent also employed verification codes and complaint forms, which would allow users to recover stolen identity numbers.

Ma wanted to put an end to the problem of identity theft, but knew that solving the issue could mean inconveniencing users, through the use of more registration restrictions and added forms of user validation. Despite the fact that there seemed to be a great potential for a negative impact associated with using more rigorous security measures, he hoped that legislation could be promulgated to improve information security.

Indeed, with the problem showing no sign of abating, Ma decided to take strong retaliatory action. Tencent used a combination of technical means and judicial powers for the counterattack, increasing the frequency of verification code protection and other means designed to effectively deter and prevent theft.

With keyloggers and trojans running rampant, Tencent introduced 'nProtect' encryption technology. They publicly announced that they would continue to use legal means to crack down on identity theft. In addition, Ma reminded customers not to run programs of unknown origin and to remain wary of QQ news from non-Tencent websites, as these were easy avenues for criminals to exploit.

There was also an intellectual property issue: in recent years, violations of intellectual property involving high-tech enterprises and infringement of commercial secrets had gained greater attention.

Ma stated during an interview with *Chinese Entrepreneurs* that: "Part of Tencent's connection with netizens was supporting security and cooperating with public security and other organs. One group we caught stealing was comprised of more than ten people in Guangdong, the largest case to date. It took nine months to uncover, but saved us a lot of trouble later on. It also made me realize that many young people do not realize that stealing virtual goods is a crime, and so we have to put more effort into policing it. What I'm most worried about now is network security, and I believe that now what we have is absolutely first-class protection against account theft."

There was still a long way to go in fighting identity theft. It was a game of cat and mouse that would be difficult for Tencent to avoid as it continued developing.

CONTROVERSY OVER PAID REGISTRATION

After QQ entered people's lives, it became one of the first sites that users would log on to after turning on their computer. Its convenience hinged on the fact that users could chat online and transfer files online and offline; business owners could use QQ mailbox; and there were applications such as QQ games, QQ music and 'QQ Farm', producing a large number of dependent users.

The question still remained: if QQ were one day to become a paid service, who would use it? Although users found the notion strange, in 2001, many new users had begun to consider the idea.

With the 2000 NASDAQ stock market crash, global internet companies faced the internet winter, followed by a domino effect, which resulted in the decline of the IT industry, as sectors across the market faced turmoil. At that time, Ma was considering other ways in which Tencent could make money.

In conventional economics, the diminishing of marginal benefits is usually gradual, but this was not the case for the internet. Areas that had remained static for long periods would, at the moment of reaching a tipping point, suddenly see a dramatic surge as their benefits revealed themselves.

So it was for Ma's little penguin: in the middle of 2001, Tencent's user base increased rapidly, straining operations.

In desperation, Ma began to control user registration. Since February 2001 it had become increasingly difficult to limit user registration, and large numbers of new users joined every day.

Ma was uncomfortable because Tencent's monthly expenses were around ¥2 million, of which three quarters could be attributed to increases in the cost of equipment. By March 2002, Ma attempted to launch a new service selling QQ registrations. In September 2002, in order to control the surge in users, he officially launched paid registration at ¥2 a month, halting free QQ registration and one-off numbers. By November of the same year, QQ issued legal warnings, banning the sale of QQ numbers.

At the end of 2002, the news arrived that broke users' hearts: free numbers and certain paid numbers were to be halted, leaving users the option of applications for numbers with bimonthly charges.

Chinese internet users had become accustomed to free access to resources and information from the internet, and expressed hurt at Tencent's actions. It was reported that, having lived with pop-ups and flashing window ads, the reality of being faced with this method of increasing revenue seemed unfair.

At the time, it was not only QQ's netizens who opposed the changes, but the media as well. Tencent issued a statement on 22 August of that year, noting that they were limiting registration because some users had registered more than one QQ number, taking up a considerable share of resources. He reinforced that the company had also shown a great deal of restraint, hoping to avoid upsetting users and hoping for a win-win situation.

Ma was entitled to unilaterally carry out reform, with users having the ability to accept, or to decline any changes by exiting.

In May 2002, rumours circulated around the internet that QQ would become a paid service. By July, Ma gave a telephone interview in which he said that the fee would only apply to new users, with a ¥10 per month option for some.

Ma explained that the changes were all part of an overall strategy of development, and that, for newly registered users, Tencent would increase the number of services, such as password protection, to give them peace of mind. In addition, Ma said he would maintain free registration and open up more overseas accounts.

In June 2003, Ma sent a message across mobile services that, for their third birthday, they would be offering long-term free QQ numbers.

In August 2003, QQ once again opened free registration to users, but based it upon the condition that users could not go longer than seven days without logging in. This was changed to one week, then a month, then three months. In the end, the restriction only applied to malicious registrations.

These policy adjustments were born of Ma's awareness of Tencent's need to supplement its meagre sources of income with registration fees, but did not compensate for the loss of users, making Ma more determined to strengthen his model.

In May 2010, Tencent's business model was different from other companies, and involved offering a number of free services for its more than 500 million active users. Covering billions of China's internet users, Tencent planned to develop value-added services as its main source of income.

Ma's plan for his business model, even on a global scale, was unique. It would later come to be known as 'Pony Ma's code'.

The essence of this code was to divide the services into two parts, one representing Tencent's underlying business, and the other its diverse and high-end value-added services.

THE CORAL INCIDENT

In 2006, for internet users and companies alike, the situation was tumultuous: there was rogue software across the internet, online trading had taken off, and celebrity blogs had become a focus of attention.

As always, Ma was working on updates to QQ, putting the finishing touches to Coral QQ. Yet its creator, Chen Shoufu, could not have imagined the disasters that would follow.

Coral QQ was third-party software, based on Tencent's QQ programme, which included a complete coral integrated installation kit that did not modify QQ's source code.

Its main developer was Professor Chen Shoufu at the Beijing Polytechnic University Computing Centre. In 2003, he was contacted by Tencent, who warned him about copyright issues regarding the software. They later reached a written guarantee, in which he promised to close the website which hosted his modified version of QQ's software download service, to delete all content connected with the modified software, and not to make any modifications to QQ's software in the future. On the surface, this brought an end to the feud with Tencent. However, the plugin, able to avoid copyright issues, was capable of exploring past information and continuing to study QQ's software.

Coral QQ had many interesting variant features compared to QQ: it could display a friend's IP address and location, as well as block Tencent's ads from appearing; it also contained MSN-style voice prompts for installation, and a wealth of customisation features.

Owing to these features, Coral QQ gained popularity with users. With each new update, it caught the attention of both new and old clients, providing Chen Shoufu with an online market.

Yet there was nothing Ma could do: because it did not modify any of QQ's existing programs, it was able to avoid related copyright issues. It drew a large number of downloads and, judging from the data of some websites, it was being downloaded even more than QQ.

Chen Shoufu had found each new QQ update daily dull and boring, but, guided by innovative, outside-the-box thinking, and GAIM and Luma QQ, he found a way to develop QQ 4.0.

With Coral being continuously renewed and developed, Ma felt he could not sit idly by. Around September 2006, Chen Shoufu was formally accused of copyright infringement and unfair competition. The court ruled against him. It drew attention, including from others borrowing from QQ's software. But it appeared that they were disappointed. Ma showed a tough stance against the problem, even refusing an out-of-court settlement, apparently in order to make an example.

The gloves were off for Ma; Coral had hit Tencent's interests. Third-party hosts of QQ had caused them to lose users and survived without QQ's advertising. For Ma, although QQ's client advertising was not the company's main project, it affected Tencent and the advertisers' interests. In addition, some copies of QQ were bundled with unauthorized software that hurt the company's reputation in the eyes of users who downloaded it. Coral QQ was the big fish they had to pursue.

Yet, even with the knowledge that revising QQ software was in violation of Tencent's intellectual property, why did so many third parties continue to do it? The answer was simple: for profit.

Coral profited through the software bundled with its version of QQ, and targeted some of the internet's most popular software. With China's countless internet users, all it took was a few hundred thousand people to download the software to make tens of thousands of yuan. A software as popular as Coral QQ was believed to have seen millions of downloads.

It was clear that the lawsuit against Chen Shoufu impacted other third-party developers. The only two well-known ones were Coral QQ and Floating Cloud QQ, and others were using Coral QQ's enhanced package to make changes of their own. If Coral QQ did not update, other software authors would turn to other versions.

Chen Shoufu was sentenced to three years in jail for copyright infringement, with ¥17 million being recovered and a ¥1.2 million fine being levied, the total reaching ¥2.37 million.

The popular generation of Coral QQ had come to an end.

Following the trial, Floating Cloud QQ also realized that they couldn't continue, and on 10 November 2007 their founders 'RunJin' and 'Crazy Gentleman' announced their withdrawal from the development of Floating Cloud. Of course, there were other third-party QQ authors continuing down their predecessors' road, but their odds of development were bleak. If Tencent's interests were affected, Ma had made it clear that he would be relentless in protecting his company.

In fact, Tencent was able to get back to basics. The third-party modifications often hid security risks, and the little penguin's powerlessness had attracted those willing to take advantage.

ANTITRUST AND GAMBLING CONTROVERSY

Having grown into such a large internet company, Tencent inevitably began to face issues familiar to any large business, such as having a monopoly and numerous imitators.

In May 2006, Tencent filed a lawsuit with the Beijing Municipal First Intermediate People's Court claiming that a significant decline in Tencent's mobile instant messaging users had occurred since July 2005 as a result of the Zhangzhong Company's PICA software.

Zhangzhong was founded in 2004 as a mobile multimedia communication services and information technology company. In early 2005, the company introduced PICE, a piece of software through which users could log onto QQ, and which greatly resembled it.

After investigating a decline in its number of registered users, Tencent discovered that Zhangzhong had been 'working from within' and took them to court for copyright violations of their software.

Ma, not wanting to draw media attention, did not make a public announcement. However, in May 2006, five months after bringing the action, Zhangzhong brought a counter-action, accusing Tencent of monopolisation and unfair competition, and thus attracting media coverage.

Zhangzhong stated in their allegations that Tencent's rates were deliberately set in order to hinder other communications companies, and that this was in clear breach of the *Telecommunications Ordinance*, which stated that it was illegal to "refuse to connect with other telecommunication operators", as well as unfair competition laws that stated "Operators should operate in good faith and comply with recognized principles of commercial practice".

In addition, Zhangzhong indicated that Tencent had employed various means to exert pressure on competitors, including Zhangzhong itself, thus thwarting their business.

What Zhangzhong sought was greater interconnectivity, such as that seen between companies like Yahoo Messenger and MSN. But Ma would not admit defeat.

In court, Tencent stated that if other companies wished to operate with Tencent, Tencent would need to first consider their own users and their reaction, and act fairly and impartially regarding the implementation of any cooperation plans.

The Beijing Municipal First Intermediate People's Court upheld Tencent's claim against Zhangzhong's PICA, awarding ¥2 million compensation. Although Tencent had won, and pledged to participate more openly and cooperatively in the market, the result could not really be said to be either a positive or negative step for the company.

The lawsuit ended in February 2007, when the company ran into yet another problem.

In July 2006, an anonymous article had appeared online: *An open letter to Shenzhen's municipal officials regarding Tencent's alleged gambling.*

Gambling? For Tencent, this was no trivial matter. Within a number of months, TV programmes were focusing on issues such as the suggestion that Tencent's QQ coins, a virtual currency that could be used to purchase goods and services, were a disguised form of online gambling.

QQ's games, such as 21 and five-card stud, required a certain amount of points, a virtual currency, which could be accumulated by winning games, or awarded in Q coin exchanges.

One coin of virtual currency had a value equivalent to one yuan of actual money, and thus led to people suggesting that, even if it could only be used online, given its equivalence to real world currency, how could gambling online be said to be different to real-life gambling?

One yuan could be used in games to purchase 10,000 online coins, while hundreds of yuan could make you a millionaire in the game, rendering it an online marketplace. Behind the hundreds and thousands and millions of game currency being traded in acts of virtual 'deal or no deal', currency amounts were also rising, conveying money into the pockets of Tencent.

After winning currency in games, players could exchange it for Q coins to buy online products or services from Tencent. These prices were higher than they would be in a real-world marketplace. For example, gamers could use virtual currency in order to buy a phone, and essentially, although they were spending actual money, it never felt as if they were directly doing so – this was the genius of Tencent.

In addition, Tencent received a percentage cut from every deal gamers made. For example, if two players were engaged in a game and one lost a million, another player would take this amount; but Tencent would extract 10% as a charge for playing, so that the winner only received 900,000 in virtual game currency.

The problem lay in the fact that there were no limits on Tencent's games or need to invest capital, and that the company was using 'disguised' renminbi to encourage players to gamble. The news hit websites, following the release of the anonymous letters: *Tencent's Gambling Problem*. CCTV also covered the story, along with the rest of the media.

After CCTV's intervention, Tencent shut down the gambling in an attempt to halt the black market, announcing that game currency could no longer be exchanged for Q coins. The barrage of reports on the issue had proved something of a blessing in disguise for Tencent, insofar as it helped them recognize and resolve the problem.

WAGE CUTS

Although Ma conducted his business with care and caution, some confrontation was unavoidable. One such example was when he faced a battle with Tencent's old rival, MSN.

One day in 2006, a post appeared online describing imminent redundancies at Tencent; the website posting the article claimed to have received an email from Ma describing a change from quarterly to yearly bonuses for employees. In addition, it alleged that Tencent had fired 5% of their lowest-performing staff. The author of the post wrote that Tencent's development was slipping behind compared to previous years, and that their share options lacked value.

The post set off a firestorm on the internet. But what on earth had prompted it?

Tencent may have believed it to be retribution for poaching MSN's employees, including MSN's Xiong Minghua. Previous to the online allegations, Ma had developed the idea of a new pay system, as well as the idea of losing 5% of all underperforming employees. The pay system substituted quarterly awards with yearly bonuses, in order to avoid having employees take their quarterly award and then leave the company. The 5% firing system was intended to foster a competitive environment, which would encourage innovation within the company.

But the leaked email meant that, with Ma not having yet announced the new policy, and internal complaints from Tencent's employees, his plans were disrupted.

Ma understood clearly that, if the situation persisted, it would shake morale and encourage MSN's intervention. Yet the reforms were not particularly radical: one was aimed at retaining talent, and the other at encouraging Tencent to do more. It was not intended to be viewed as a strategy for increasing staff layoffs.

Ma issued a public statement, stressing that the policies were not intended as layoffs, but to develop the company and improve it, so that it might become competitive internationally.

Tencent was let off the hook, and tensions finally died down. Ma's calm attitude and swift reaction plus his quiet leadership, helped strengthen the company's further development.

ONLINE FRAUD

There is an old Chinese idiom which states: 'tall trees attract wind'. With Ma having turned the Tencent penguin into a giant, there was little doubt the wind would come.

With the increasing number of QQ users, Tencent's network had become a target for criminals and one of the biggest victims of cybercrime. Tencent's 2006 report highlighted users' online safety as a top priority.

In December 2005, Ma told *China News Weekly*: "Looking at the internet as a whole, there are good and bad aspects. We put in a great deal of effort, but as in offline society, there will always be cases of people taking advantage of human fallibilities and weaknesses, such as when winning someone's trust before cheating them. This is not a technical problem, but a communication problem, and one that reflects real-life society."

It was true that Tencent was simply a communication platform: Ma provided a tool for internet users and operators providing mail services. The content of messages was not directly regulated, and technical measures were thus limited to restrictions on areas such as bulk and junk mail.

Although it was difficult for Ma to monitor all content, Tencent spared no effort in educating users about how to protect themselves. QQ's interface contained a prominent dialogue box reminding users of various tricks and scams of which they should be wary. In addition, Ma had adopted a series of technical upgrades and optimization services, further enhancing QQ's security.

In March 2007, Ma participated in a conference on the internet and protection of intellectual property rights, where he stated that, "We are now exposed to cybercrimes that involve stalking user accounts in ways that both disrupt online networks and users' lives. The problem is difficult to control and has causes emanating from society, the legal system, technology, management and education. At present, the law often results in wrongful convictions or sentences that are too lenient, thus failing in its aims of due punishment and deterrence. At the same time, there is no established moral system online or educational guidance, and offenders like hackers and those who produce viruses are seen as technological geniuses – an unfortunate direction for society to travel in."

On 8 January 2007, to combat cyber theft, Ma joined NetEase, Kingsoft, Shanda, Nine Cities and four other well-known network service providers aimed at targeting and reducing cyber theft. They issued a statement expressing their hope that cyber theft could be punished severely, to protect the security of users online. Ma expressed his wish – along with others who shared his concerns – that the problem could be managed.

Tencent's operation focused on network security, stability and quality, with security taking top priority. To this end, Ma worked with antivirus developers to build QQ Security Centre. They also collaborated with national security agencies to crack down on malicious websites. In order to ensure stable, reliable services, he also established a 24hour watch centre that could respond at the first sign of anything unusual.

In order to help guide users through newly established security requirements, Ma created a virtual online course. It used network case studies, combined with a variety of personalised online courses – as well as a touch of humour – to teach users about QQ-related security issues and how to confront them.

3Q WAR: DIFFERING OPINIONS

During the Spring Festival of 2010, Tencent upgraded QQ with QQ Doctor, a security protection software. It was a move that would prove difficult to forget for Qihu360's older employees.

In May 2010, QQ Doctor became QQ Computer Protection. The software was very similar to Qihu360's. During the Mid-Autumn Festival later in the year, Tencent rolled the software out to users in second and third-tier cities.

The move was particularly worrying precisely because QQ had a history of creating programs that became universal, killing off similar competitors, such as QQ Farm and QQ Chinese. Would Qihu360 encounter a similar fate?

On 27 September, Qihu360 released software designed to monitor violations of user privacy, which resulted in claims that QQ had indeed breached users' privacy. Tencent denied the claim and asserted that Qihu360's software had been improperly promoted.

Unwilling to see their market share taken by QQ, Qihu360 decided to develop a new program at the end of September that year. The software was promoted as allowing users to filter QQ's advertising.

The result made a serious impact on the foundations of Tencent's business model. By 3 November, a representative for Tencent released a message to its users that became famous: either use 360's software to uninstall QQ, or let QQ delete 360's software.

The two companies had gone from silent confrontation to war: the '3Q War'.

Faced with the brutal alternatives, many users were forced to delete 360's software. In their view, for all the benefits of antivirus software, the ease and habituated use they had developed around QQ was far greater.

Within a day, 20% of users had uninstalled 360's software. At 200 million installations, this meant that, overnight, 40 million users had uninstalled it. But there was also a backlash, with netizens adopting slogans advocating loyalty to the software. In November, with the formal involvement of officials in the 3Q War, the two companies reached an agreement, with Qihu360 publicly apologizing and the two pieces of software being rendered compatible.

It must be acknowledged that, for Ma, the freedom he enjoys today was won at the hard-earned price of the many trials that Tencent went through in its earlier days. It is also crucial to recognize that for any enterprise, a period of growth and development will always result in a degree of confrontation with rival companies.

On 14 October 2000, Tencent sued Qihu360 for unfair competition. In April 2011, the court awarded a judgment ordering Qihu360 pay Tencent ¥400,000 in compensation. Then, in June, another suit against the company saw Tencent awarded ¥5 million in compensation. In October, Qihu360 sued Tencent for abusing its dominant market position, but lost and was forced to bear the costs of the lawsuit.

Insiders saw the process of the 3Q War as being far more important than its result. In this long war, Qihu360's battle for survival could be seen as a challenge to the internet giant. Had there been no confrontation, Ma would likely have continued his 'imitation and bundle with pre-existing services' mode of operation. This may have meant neglecting to focus on the larger user experience. Fortunately, through the vagaries of the 3Q War, the company became more aware of user demands and adjusted their business strategies accordingly.

CHAPTER

THE PENGUIN
WAS BORN RICH

Monternet was a gift for Tencent, with Ma playing the roles of both explorer and beneficiary. He had the keen instincts of an entrepreneur and the gift of business opportunities. Along the road to building the penguin empire, of all the gifts that they had received, the greatest was Monternet.

Monternet, as previously mentioned, was a service provider. It offered services directly for mobile internet operators. Such business could be divided into two major classes: the first being a portal service provider, delivering ringtones, pictures, news and games to portal websites; the second class was a professional service provider, which offered more tailored services and had the advantage of being continually innovative and creative.

In addition, there was a special type of service provider, of which Tencent was an example. Unlike traditional SMS service providers, Tencent did not have ordinary pictures, ring tones, games and other services, but focused mainly on services specific to QQ and text messages relating to the QQ platform.

In April 2000, Tencent had over 5 million registered users, with more than 100,000 users simultaneously on-line in May; by June, this had risen to over 10 million registered users.

In August of that year, many sites disappeared from the internet, as the dotcom bubble burst. Just as the collective disaster – and ensuing consternation – was beginning to erupt, Ma and Guangdong Mobile signed cooperation agreements with China Mobile, which would allow QQ and Guangdong Mobile users to send and receive text messages anywhere, anytime.

In April 2001, when China Mobile decided to settle its bills with its service providers, Ma had accumulated six months of experience, and the Monternet business plan had saved him and his fledgling company. In competition with many other content providers, Ma was able, by virtue of Mobile QQ, to carve out a space.

Mobile QQ took full advantage of the services of mobile communication operators, in order to offer mobile users the opportunity to communicate directly with QQ users using SMS. It can be said that Mobile QQ was the first example in the history of 3G internet.

In 2001, through the active efforts of Ma, Tencent had established partnerships with telecommunications operators all over China. Ma said that their approach in the beginning had been to rely on wireless value-added services, including Mobile QQ, because Monternet had not yet appeared.

In fact, when China Mobile initially launched the Monternet service, it did not think this innovative mobile internet service could actually ultimately save online companies.

From the first day that Mobile QQ was launched, Ma worked continuously on improving the user experience. In November 2002, at a conference in Hangzhou, Ma said of Mobile QQ's future: "We have, with China Mobile, just released an SMS service that allows you to send images through your mobile, and we have many other services planned for the future. These will allow the mobile to act as if it were a computer and diversify its functions." In this, we can see that Tencent had become the backbone of China Mobile's Monternet, and its shares in Monternet accounted for 70% of the total.

In 2003, Ma felt that, from the point of view of wireless business development, Tencent's wireless business and value-added services had found suitable models. Through continuous exploration and improvement, they had created a wide variety of services, whether for entertainment, dating or games. Later, with the launch of the Dynamic Zone brand, Ma's wireless data services discovered a new direction.

Regardless of whether the cooperation with telecom operators was happy or not, Mobile QQ brought huge profits to Ma: over a long period it accounted for around half of all profit made. China Mobile used QQ Mobile to add value to its own services. However, as China Mobile had begun progressing to become an expert in mobile messaging, they had developed Fetion, a service that, by 2006, was gradually maturing.

China Mobile hoped to move millions of QQ users to Fetion, but this was not good news for Ma: QQ accounted for 60% of the market share in the mobile instant messaging market, and he was unwilling to share their 7 million QQ users with others.

To the surprise of some in the industry, on 29 December 2006, China Mobile ended all its partnerships with service providers in wireless instant messaging. In Hong Kong, Ma announced that they would cooperate with Fetion, and QQ users would transition to the platform. Naturally, Tencent and China Mobile's agreement was to be extended for half a year.

By 2008, millions of users were on Fetion QQ. In order to maintain growth, China Mobile continued to cooperate with Tencent. However, with the development of Fetion, China Mobile inevitably found mobile revenues growing, and so Tencent changed plans to avoid conflict with China Mobile. It chose, instead, to try and expand its revenue.

Not long after, a software called WeChat was created. It would prove to be an unprecedented success in the telecommunications industry

THE SUDDEN EMERGENCE OF WECHAT

On 21 January 2011, Tencent launched WeChat, an app specifically designed as a one-stop free instant messaging service. It was unaffected by problems regarding internet traffic while connecting to online platforms, and also allowed users to form groups, search for nearby users, and offered other, additional services.

Once the app was launched it was immediately taken up by mobile users of all ages. On 29 March 2012, the number of users broke through the 100 million mark.

It had taken just 433 days.

Many app makers were worried by WeChat's success. Since the 3Q War, Ma had advocated openness as the lever for Tencent's development. Of course, this was not 'openness' in some general, literal sense, but rather an openness of attitude and thinking, such that all the various elements people associated with the internet could be combined together.

Ma believed that the internationalization of China's internet companies had not succeeded. "In the past," he said, "China's internet models were copied from the US, and were therefore unlikely to be taken up overseas. As the mobile internet wave swept the world, many were unready or limited by existing PC or other services, making it difficult to create mobile-specific products. Now that mobile internet and phone development is faster here, to some extent, than the West, Chinese companies have a massive opportunity."

WeChat had become a tool with which Ma could scope out the prospects of internationalization. Ma believed that WeChat's small innovations were faster than those in Europe and America, such as their use of open platforms and friendship circles. These were all original to Tencent, and far ahead of what they had previously achieved.

The rapid rise of apps posed a huge challenge to traditional services, leading to WeChat's 'fee charging incidents'.

From the end of February 2013, rumours started among telecom operators that WeChat would charge fees. On 31 March, Telecommunications Minister Miao Wei, in the second 'Forum in Lingnan', mentioned that they would support telecom operators. However, after the announcement was made, it was immediately opposed by the majority of users, who saw it as double charging, since they already paid for internet and traffic fees. On 23 April 2013, a spokesperson again stated that charges for new services, such as the internet, would be decided by the market, and not the government.

After that, the furore over WeChat charging fees temporarily died down.

Although falling income had compelled Ma to introduce the idea of charging for WeChat, it was met with opposition from users. Ma understood that WeChat's relationship with telecom operators was sensitive; however, he knew that what WeChat offered was a fundamentally different service, and that, as a result, its future development would lean towards cooperation rather than conflict.

A PRINTING FACTORY FOR ONLINE CURRENCY

From a small penguin to a veritable local kingpin, Tencent had not only gained the ability to turn a profit, but had added a new function: selling Q coins.

Q coins were worth ¥1 each, and were used to pay for services such as QQ numbers and QQ membership.

Some believed that Q coins could impact China's financial order, on the basis that, whereas the yuan was a limited statutory currency, Q coins were virtual and unlimited, so they might be capable of replacing the yuan as an online trading currency. It was also noted that large bets were made on QQ games, and because the virtual currency was freely convertible, QQ coins, to some extent, carried an element of black market currency about them.

In reality, Q coins were merely intended for purchasing Tencent's value-added services, and could not cross over into the wider financial system. Tencent's policy was that Q coins were a one-way exchange: once a user had purchased Q currency, it could not be converted back into yuan.

The popularity of Q coins was also inextricably linked to the lack of alternative online payment methods in the internet's early days. At that time, gamers purchasing equipment in a game could only use a bank transfer, which was potentially troublesome, because purchasing equipment in a game usually required time for negotiations. Thus, the Q coin gradually replaced the traditional financial means of exchange. Q coins could also be gained as bonuses in online forums, exchanged for goods, or used to pay for advertising.

With regard to the worries of experts about the potential of Q coins replacing the yuan as an online currency, some users found their fears somewhat alarmist, given that Q coins were not freely convertible. Generally, other than in cases where an exchange took place face to face in the same city, transactions across different cities required mutual trust in the security of the website being used.

If Q coins were so favoured by users, how many of them did Tencent distribute? It is impossible to calculate a figure, since no record was ever kept.

According to financial definitions, currency represents a special fixed means of exchange. Only the yuan met this definition, so how did Q coins become a virtual currency circulated online?

Some experts felt that Q coins could not be considered a virtual currency, but a symbol recognized online by netizens, because the yuan did not follow the value of the Q coin in the market; it had no connection to the national financial system.

Nevertheless, some people believed that the Q coin was already a type of embryonic currency; so long as Tencent had potential, the possibility of a Q coin currency was not impossible.

Today, there are many virtual currencies. Due to a gap in the law, there are few regulatory measures that can be taken against them, and their circulation remains undocumented. Some have boldly predicted that the phenomenon is likely to lead to inflation and infringe upon users' interests, causing them to lose confidence in internet transactions.

Owing to fears surrounding this idea, some lawyers felt the Central Bank ought to strictly regulate the issuing of qualification necessary to trade in virtual currency.

Ma also adjusted the company's policy on Q coins, preventing them from being exchanged into gaming currency; instead, gaming currency could only be used to buy items within games. Online trafficking in Q coins usually involved stolen accounts, something Ma was determined to resist. Tencent was also enhancing its technology to combat disturbing online virtual trading.

THE JOY OF VALUE-ADDED SERVICES

Along with the discussion of Q coins among commentators, Tencent was also seeing an increase in virtual goods, a symbol of netizens' frenzied quest for virtual services in the online age. Ma seized the opportunity.

QQ's largest virtual service was QQ Show. One day in 2002, a company product manager named Xu Liang accidentally happened across a game within Korea online. The game was called *Avatar*. The game allowed users to design virtual personalities with hair, clothing, facial expressions, and many other features, and to pay for the customization. Xu Liang realized that the use of virtual avatars on QQ could represent a new and profitable channel for the company.

The term 'avatar' originates in India from the Sanskrit. It refers to the manifestation of a deity or released soul in bodily form. Online, its meaning had become synonymous with the use of virtual images and characters to represent people.

Ma saw a great deal of potential in Xu Liang's idea. A service such as QQ Show could help users to engage on a more personal level with QQ, and also created a way for users to give themselves a more 'human' face and personality online.

Although Ma had confidence in the idea, he was not someone who would blindly follow trends or unwarranted innovation, and wished to learn best practice before attempting to go beyond it. In order to allow Tencent to continue developing, Ma believed in exploring various options multiple times, and finally discovered that Korea and China had a greater cultural similarity than China did with

Europe and America, thus making it a more stable long-term frame of reference.

In January 2003, QQ Show was officially launched. Just as in the fashion industry, where the brand a person wore could represent a kind of personal style, he wanted QQ Show to represent a user's personal taste.

Shortly after QQ Show began, Ma had international companies such as Nike offer images of their latest products and clothing online for users to download. The service was free: Tencent's user base was so large it did not have to spend a cent on the service. Eventually, Ma asked the big companies for advertising, and they wasted no time in supplying it. QQ Show was reaping huge benefits.

Ma also used QQ Show to partner with the entertainment industry. In 2005, Tencent promoted Chen Kaige's film *The Promise* on QQ Show. As more and more people engaged in life online, it became increasingly important to meet the recreational needs of users, of which film and television was one of the most important aspects.

With QQ Show as the original example, Ma felt he had found an offline value-added business model, which he described as "online value-added services". He proceeded to launch other services in this vein, such as Qzone and QQ Pet.

The appearance of QQ Space marked the birth of China's first large profitable blogging service. Although it was a free service, many users were willing to pay extra in order to customise their templates, thereby providing profit for QQ.

Compared with QQ Show, QQ Space's ability to make money was greater. The former could only sell clothes and backgrounds, while QQ Space could sell anything and everything.

Thanks to Ma, Tencent had developed a wide range of value-added services and new businesses, such as online games. Ma believed these could be used to help retain users and that online games would help the company's brand to become more attractive.

QQ IN THE PRESENT: A LIFE WITHOUT QQ?

Since its launch, QQ had become an indispensable part of people's lives. With the development of technology, it had become a virtual address book for many users, as well as a hub for connecting people.

In order to meet public demand, Ma had continually updated the software, allowing it to become stronger and stronger. More features were introduced, in order to meet people's desire for new services.

According to surveys, QQ was, after telephone and mobile services, the third largest communication tool in China, and its frequency of use outpaced even those. Whether people were willing to admit it or not, QQ had become an indispensible part of people's lives.

WECHAT WILL CHANGE YOUR LIFE

With the ongoing universalization of the WeChat platform, more and more businesses were becoming aware of its opportunities and the effect it was having on people's lives, from booking taxis to finding jobs and shopping. WeChat payments were also more convenient for those away from their PC: its scanning technology allowed for ease of shopping and job applications.

However, online shopping had also brought an increase in fake goods, rising prices and post-sale issues, as well as items being damaged during postal transit, a problem for both sellers and buyers. Thus, physical purchases continued to remain a part of people's buying habits.

With the growing popularity of scanning technology, many consumers adopted new buying patterns, picking up their phone to scan products for relevant information, even finding out whether the product had a fake counterpart or not. It changed the experience of shopping at local businesses.

Although there were still problems of confidentiality and authenticity of information, it was believed that improvement would lead to more systematic and scientific security systems and means of network authentication.

WeChat had many advantages over QQ: the fact that photos and video could be transmitted almost instantaneously to one's circle of friends, rather than requiring a PC as intermediary, was one such example. Moreover, the real-time Twitter-like friend feed gave people a sense of real-life activity, and of being part of a living and vibrant community.

Certainly WeChat had flaws as well, particularly in the way it could create a 'capsule effect' or echo chamber for the user, in which a person's feed might revolve solely around a limited number of issues or lifestyles, even to the point where multiple people would post and repeat the same news, restricting people's ability to think more widely or broadly.

As WeChat's popularity broadened, so did people's dependence on their mobiles: the sight of friends meeting, only to end up sitting together while staring at their phones, became a common occurrence. In this trend, some people saw the end of 'real' human interaction, in favour of strangers, who were made to seem closer than they really were. But others believed it was just a sign of changing times, and not a cause for thinking that social collapse was inevitable.

A topic of endless discussion and controversy, the only thing people could be sure of was that, whether you used the app or not, WeChat was always close by.

THE STORY OF THE LITTLE PENGUIN'S MOTHER AND FATHER

For all his technical talent, Ma was, at heart, a senior geek who learned from the internet as a user, regularly spending at least three hours a day online and, at his most obsessed, more than ten hours a day. Later, as the business of Tencent took up more of his time, he was only able to spend about an hour online.

Being very focused and professionally driven, Ma had little time for love and dating. It had possibly never occurred to him that his little penguin could function as a matchmaker.

One day in May 2004, Tencent's Hong Kong employees went to Shenzhen on exchange, as they did not use QQ and he wanted other employees to teach them how it functioned. For added convenience, he opened the limit on the number of friends a person could add, so that people could freely add him.

One of those who added him was a girl he had never met. The girl had casually asked him, "Hey! Who are you?" He nonchalantly replied, "The father of the penguin." She took up the joke and said, "Then I am the penguin's mother."

She introduced herself as Wang Danting, a young lecturer at Harbin Normal University.

Three months later, Ma went to Beijing on business. Coincidentally, Wang was also travelling to Beijing to attend a concert. When they crossed paths and she saw his business card, she realized he truly was the "father of the penguin". Her impression of him was that he possessed real honesty, as well as being gentle and well mannered.

Ma and Wang spent their honeymoon in Shenzhen. Though the landscape was charming, the man-made lake contained a lot of mosquitoes that often bit Wang. Ma hired workers to fill in the lake, turning it into a large garden. Later, Wang planted a host of fruit trees in the garden, such as peaches and grapes.

After marrying, Ma underwent some major changes. Previously he had worked until midnight every day, searching for problems that he would then try to fix with other staff. Now, he came home from work around 9pm. Nonetheless, he remained a workaholic – employees would inevitably find suggestions in their inbox each morning, which had been sent around 11pm or so the previous night.

Another change was in Ma's physical appearance: under Wang's guidance he had begun to pay more attention to his manner and dress, his public appearances becoming more confident, stylish and relaxed. Wang was his rock, the source of his happiness. Marrying her had brought new vigour to his life. Wang was smart, kind and considerate. And she loved Ma, a love that lifted them up, even as they depended upon it to continually fill their lives with happiness.

CHAPTER

THE DECISIVE BATTLE
BEGAN AT THE TOP OF
THE MOUNTAIN
OF INSTANT
TELECOMMUNICATION

BROTHER MA'S MERCY AIDS A TIGER

While Ma's little penguins were becoming the new stars of China's internet world, an instant messaging service from abroad had entered the battle: MSN.

MSN was created by Microsoft. It appeared on 24 August 1995, with the release of Windows 95. It was available as a free download from Hotmail and included chat, video and incoming mail functions, among others.

Compared to Ma's QQ, the advantage of MSN was that it was perfectly combined with Windows, so users did not have to worry about hard disc space when installing MSN (during the 1990s, having extra hard disk capacity was a major advantage). Since 90% of China's PC users employed Microsoft, MSN was warmly welcomed.

In fact, Microsoft's decision to combine MSN with its operating system was seen by people in Europe and the US as constituting a monopoly. The case found its way into the courts, where it was depicted as a blatant contravention of user rights. Though this deterred Microsoft somewhat, Ma himself had no such awareness of antitrust law – if he had, he might have taken legal action against Microsoft directly.

In October 2001, Microsoft went further, launching a mainland version of MSN, bundled with a Chinese version of the link to MSN's portal: china.msn.com. Clearly, Microsoft was attempting to make inroads into the large Chinese market.

The Chinese version of the MSN website was hosted in the US. Microsoft's MSN division General Manager for Asia explained: "China places more stringent restrictions on foreign internet content providers, so we hoped, in this way, to avoid running into regulatory trouble."

Microsoft moved without warning, and Ma and other instant messaging software companies did not know what to do. Although there had been media rumours of MSN China's ambitions, these had all been denied by Microsoft. It seemed they had planned to reach deep into the market and had no intention of easily giving away their plans, thus protecting themselves from competition.

Ma showed no panic, saying simply that, "Pressure is a good thing – we won't fight recklessly."

On 24 October 2002, with Bill Gates having participated in the official ceremony for MSN 8.0's release in Canada and the US, held at Central Park in New York, the General Manager of MSN Asia came to Beijing to meet with the media, completing the initial Chinese promotions of MSN.

The visit saw many speculate that Microsoft would accelerate the speed of its entry into the Chinese market. Once again, this speculation was denied by Microsoft.

Although Microsoft attempted to be circumspect about their plans for MSN, one fact remained hard to deny, and that was that MSN had become the preferred software of China's businesspeople and intellectuals. Along with this positive reception, Microsoft was continually improving MSN, releasing MSN Messenger 7.0 on 7 April 2005.

MSN's spears were directly aimed at Ma's little penguin. Compared with QQ, MSN Messenger 7.0 had many bright spots, which Microsoft had repeatedly emphasized. MSN allowed the users to show both their real name and a personal message, where they could express themselves more uniquely and individually.

What made Ma feel even more helpless was when MSN Messenger released a service similar to QQ Space: MSN Spaces, where MSN users could network through blogs, photos, music, and other fashionable modes of self-expression.

In addition to these new features, MSN's Hotmail service was also given greater stability and allowed for instant messaging across different platforms, making it almost indistinguishable from QQ.

Ma could see the situation and the folly of their inattention. He had not thought MSN would pose a threat to Tencent. But as he had been competing in the instant messaging market with Ding Lei and Chen Tianqiao, MSN China had gradually developed from a seed into a mighty tree. By the time Ma awoke, he found himself standing in its shade.

Before Microsoft announced that MSN would enter the Chinese market, he had been considering finding a partner. Online auction site eBay had just entered the market. Through an injection of funds they had established themselves in China. Microsoft, on the other hand, were simply looking for a partner to collaborate with in the Chinese market. After some investigation they settled on Shanghai Alliance Investments. The plan was to establish a joint venture that would allow MSN to enter China.

MSN was well prepared, even staving off competitors like QQ. But it could also be said that MSN's actions were based on long-term observation of QQ, and the developing scenario put the two companies on a road to facing off in the instant messaging market.

MICROSOFT'S CRUSADE

On 11 May 2005, Microsoft's internet division announced that they had set up a joint venture with Shanghai United Investments to launch MSN in China.

Ma always expected that MSN would be greeted with fanfare and that Tencent would, one day, have to compete with them, based on his observations and analyses. But the formal announcement brought a renewed pressure. Although QQ's localization gave it a certain advantage, Microsoft commanded status and power, and it was difficult to see who would outpace the other.

On 2 June 2005, staggering news broke out on the internet: nine different companies would partner with MSN. The nine partners, among China's most profitable websites, offered the most popular services and had the best outlook for development.

The press releases indicated that MSN's entry to China was one more move in a larger game. Although Ma was worried, he remained calm, because he was engaged in competition with MSN and had learned something from observing their previous behaviour and business moves. Previously, Ma had targeted users aged 20 years and under, but with MSN's arrival, he realized he would need to target high-end white-collar users in order to expand the company's user base and prevent MSN from gaining an upper hand over them.

In a televized interview, Ma said: "In the communications market, our biggest rival is MSN, but competition at present is extremely fierce, with over 40 large and small operations battling. The bars to market entry are not high, but the business is hard to learn. A company's user base is vital to value: the bigger the base, the greater the value. Thus, those who move early have a certain advantage."

Ma admitted that he had felt the pressure to survive in the face of MSN. Where could QQ assert an advantage? QQ's user base was heavily reliant on younger users. By contrast, MSN had a different position. Its messaging service was focused mainly on communications between people who knew one another, while QQ was more geared towards communicating with strangers or new acquaintances.

Before MSN's challenge, Ma had made some progress with QQ's related products. A piece of software called BQQ was created for enterprise users. After some experiments, Ma deduced that the core competitiveness of instant communication software lay in the operation of the user's zone and the community. The winner was not necessarily the company who had the most users. With enterprise users increasing, BQQ could carry over users of other instant messaging (IM) software. From this perspective, the competition with MSN was not necessarily a bad thing. So long as Tencent adopted the right strategy, it could still win over the users of MSN.

Ma reached this conclusion after an embarrassing discovery he made looking at QQ's user base. Before online gaming was popular, QQ's popularity had seen the rise of a great number of net cafes. It was a source of angst for QQ's competition, since many potential users were only aware of QQ. However, because most of those who went to net cafes were young people rather than businesspeople, QQ imperceptibly became a kind of grassroots IM software. So much so that, in some large companies, QQ was blocked and employees were not allowed to access it.

Thus, QQ appeared to stand for a divide between white-collar workers and students. This allowed MSN to enter the Chinese market and offer elegant business-targeted services. It had a viral appeal: once a business took up MSN, employees would become reliant on it.

Yet the two audiences were not entirely divided: students who grew into white-collar workers would continue to use MSN as well as QQ. Of course, using QQ was a habit, while MSN was a need. Nonetheless, MSN had certain advantages over QQ.

MSN's interface was very simple and had the huge advantage of being free of advertising; this alone was enough to shift some QQ users. In Ma's view, Tencent could not achieve MSN's advantages in the short term, as they were reliant on advertising. QQ's entertainment focus also prevented it from having the elegance of MSN and this worried Ma. Moreover, MSN had Microsoft's support, which allowed them a certain margin of error – something Tencent could not afford.

QQ therefore had to maintain its local and youth-focused qualities, for fear of losing out to Microsoft if it attempted to encroach on foreign territory. Better to wage war on a new battleground than to attempt to compete with someone more established.

With this in mind, Ma launched a brilliant counter-attack. In 2004, Ma unveiled Tencent Messenger. It was entirely designed to combat MSN. If QQ was aimed at individual users, Tencent Messenger was for business users, and adapted to the business environment every bit as fluidly as MSN.

Like QQ, Tencent Messenger was free. Users could use their phone or QQ number to register. Those who registered by phone could bind their account to that number, thus helping to ensure registered user accounts were authentic. In addition, Tencent Messenger was free of advertising and had a cleaner, less cluttered interface compared to QQ. It also included functions such as Smart Secretary, a 'yellow pages', and virtual business cards.

On 11 March 2005, Tencent acquired Foxmail and its entire team, including Zhang Xiaolong, the founder of Foxmail. Zhang had graduated in 1994 from Huazhong University with a master's degree and had long been engaged in software development and management. After joining Tencent, he immediately proved himself a strong and capable part of the team, not least in the role he played in helping to develop WeChat.

Foxmail itself was widely known because it was the only email service that could compete with Microsoft and Outlook. So why did Ma buy out Foxmail? In his words, "We liked Foxmail's technology and users." Observers believed the acquisition was intended to help discussions with Microsoft about acquiring Hotmail.

Now that the battle was heating up, Tencent and Microsoft were watching each other carefully and moving to rectify any weaknesses in their business. Tencent released Tencent Messenger 2006, which supported logins through separate email accounts, helping make the platform more open and accessible. This adjustment brought Tencent and MSN into increasingly fierce competition, as it was a clear move on Ma's part to attract users who might originally have opted to use MSN.

Although Ma had adjusted his product orientation and business strategy to claw back his position, it could be said that the new stratagem contained disadvantages as well as strengths. It was heartening and positive to observe that Tencent Messenger's user base was expanding; however, from a more negative perspective, the number of new users registering with QQ was declining. Overall, though, the strategy made sense, as Ma had recognized that MSN lacked a service that attracted the registration of new users and that Tencent Messenger did not involve the sort of advertising that was liable to irritate businesspeople. Indeed, if Tencent did not take substantial action, QQ was liable to end up becoming the plaything of young users and miss out on the professional class entirely.

In the second half of 2005, competition continued to intensify. Tencent had successfully listed in Hong Kong. MSN's Chinese web portal was developing well, but compared with local sites, it lacked the features necessary to attract more users. This factor allowed Tencent to overtake Microsoft.

However, even if Microsoft had lost momentum, they still had many powerful 'little brothers'. In response to Microsoft's wide alliance in China, Ma carried out a new idea: adjusting the layout of Tencent's web portal, and finding strategic alliances of his own.

Ma set his sights on a company called IT World Network, and contacted them in hope of organizing a partnership. They announced their strategic cooperation at a press conference in Beijing on 15 August 2005. The cooperation would cover news reviews, sales guides and markets.

Of course, this was merely a prelude to their competing with MSN, with Ma planning a new attack on a new field: one that would not leave MSN time to develop their own counterattack and would put them on the defensive.

NO INTEREST IN INTERCONNECTION

Having both worked on their strategic development, the next step for both Tencent and Microsoft was how to make a decisive strike at the other. Of course, before any large-scale attack, it was necessary to take some preparatory steps.

Microsoft moved first.

On 12 October 2005, Microsoft and Yahoo announced that there would be interconnection between MSN Messenger and Yahoo Messenger users between April 2006 and June of the same year. According to the cooperation agreement between the two companies, there would be complete interoperability between each in the second quarter of 2006, allowing a total of about 275 million users full intercommunication.

The pressure on Ma was self-evident: if China's dozens of IM companies achieved interoperability, then Tencent, left outside that circle, would be viewed by China's millions of internet users as the only barrier to achieving the dream of complete interoperability.

Indeed, Microsoft and Yahoo's cooperation was larger than he had imagined: on 13 July 2006, they published a statement saying that they would spend several months piloting the scheme and exploring the variables of interoperability. The comprehensive tests would include video, voice and wireless communications covering 350 million users across the globe.

But Microsoft and Yahoo between them did not immediately shake the dominance of Tencent in the domestic market, because Yahoo's Chinese market share was not especially high, and therefore the combined number of users on either side was not a major threat to the little penguin. Of course, this did not mean Ma could become complacent: if the rival companies took a bigger slice of the cake, then QQ's entertainment features could be overtaken by MSN. After all, among business users, the potential of IM was large.

However, from another perspective, Ma had his reasons for refusing to unite in the dream of interoperability. After all, Tencent had spent years developing its user base, and if they partnered with another IM company, they would have to share the reputation they had worked so hard to build – a fact difficult for Tencent's hardworking staff to accept. It could also damage their businesses, from online games to auctions. "We support any reasonable prospect of interconnection", Ma said, "QQ cannot unconditionally open itself and simply allow anyone to ride off the back of QQ."

On 27 October 2005, Tencent's seventh anniversary, Ma relinquished his usual low-key style to announce Tencent's latest product – the official release of QQ's 2005 edition. This was the first press conference organized specifically around the launch of new IM software since the company was founded. Ma said that, "at present, the IM industry in China has entered an era of standards."

Generally speaking, the idea of a "standard" can be interpreted in two ways: as referring to an authoritative structure or person, or to something simply being standard or customary, thereby setting an expectation. What Ma was referring to was this second meaning: he hoped for QQ to become the standard of instant messaging in the marketplace.

Ma believed that China's IM technology was a world leader, and would continue to be so as IM became more fully integrated into people's social lives. Ma quoted experts in suggesting that, "The past few years of industry development have not been standardized, but under Tencent, we will see standardization, as well as both technical and product innovation."

In a word, it was a question of who could change the standards of IM software and thus win the future of the market. Ma saw Microsoft and Yahoo's collaboration as representing a kind of test, rather than the beginning of a new standard; he summarized this point by suggesting that, "standards depend on products, products that are recognized by users and that have the ability to create industry trends. From this point of view, Tencent believes in patience and quiet dedication." This concept, that "standards depend on products", also revealed that Ma was further drifting from the idea of interconnection.

BECOME SKILLED IN STEALING FROM OTHERS

On 31 December 2005, Ma replaced Tencent's logo with an image of the Tencent QQ penguin bordered by green, yellow and red lines. With the arrival of the New Year, Ma wanted users to move past the 'Tencent = QQ' concept, and to separate their online portal and instant messaging software. The portal website was intended to show that Tencent was not simply a piece of IM software, but a combined market for e-commerce, email and a search engine service.

Ma's idea was to build a complete internet empire and create an 'online life', in which Tencent could serve as a one-stop service, catering to every user's need. To this end, Ma said: "The online portal and instant messaging depend on each other, and can overturn traditional online portals." This clearly encapsulated Ma's ideas about what an online life would look like.

Judging by the development of the industry, the future of the internet seemed likely to move in two directions: one constituted an integration of a variety of services; the other, a professional, highly specific concentration of some particular service. After some analysis, Ma decided to have Tencent walk firmly towards the first model. In Ma's words,

"The user will be able, at any time, in any place, at any terminal, and through every method of access, be able to meet their needs. Whatever they need, Tencent will provide, and everything they need will be close at hand."

Ma was building a complete network upon the internet's global highway, just as MSN had suddenly built their wall, obstructing Ma's path. Since he could not circumvent this barrier, he tried everything to tear it down, so that he could continue his plans.

On 22 December 2005, Sina Science and Technology News issued an explosive report: "Tencent had MSN's Xiong Minghua serve as senior Project Manager and co-CTO". This news immediately aroused concerns within the industry, though some believed it was all hype on the part of Tencent and did not take it to heart.

Regardless of any hype, the news revealed one crucial piece of information: the faith Ma had in his battle against MSN. Xiong Minghua joined Microsoft in 1986 and had served as a program manager. He had participated in a number of research and development projects, including Windows2000, WindowsME, and MSN, as well as gaining experience in large companies, such as IBM and KTInternational. While working in the US, Xiong had kept close contact with China's software sector, often using speeches and other opportunities to pass the world's most advanced software information onto Chinese colleagues.

From the perspective of Tencent's development prospects in China, choosing Xiong was a wise decision. They required an increasingly powerful research and development team capable of scientifically and rationally managing the development process. To this end, Ma sought out talented people. It was said that Microsoft project manager oversaw 20% of projects, showing the importance of this role. He believed Xiong's experience as a project manager could help Tencent to achieve an enhanced level of project management.

GOODBYE TO MSN

On 24 August 2014, Chinese MSN users received a letter from Microsoft's official Skype email: "The Messenger service will be closed down from 31 October in China. Don't worry, though, as your contacts will not be lost. All online communication services within the system will be moved onto Skype."

In just a few words, Microsoft's MSN was formally withdrawing from China. It had been nine years since their arrival in April 2005, and they had not managed to put an end to QQ.

When MSN had entered China, hundreds of millions of users had embraced the programs and the company had kept pace with QQ. But after an unpredictable decade of web development, Microsoft had always pursued a policy predicated on their status as a large company and had not placed enough focus on localizing MSN, thus forcing them to yield when China's smaller web companies began to push through.

All told, there were three reasons why MSN was doomed to fail. For one thing, they did not focus enough on the emerging user community: in Microsoft's view, MSN was designed to marginalize non-mainstream products, but this made it hard for their design team to obtain quality resources. Their degree of care was also lacking, leading to a waste of potential online development during the 'golden decade.' Due to a lack of localization, MSN's Chinese version was a translation of the English version and thus its many software applications were unable to meet the social needs of Chinese internet users in their online communication. Especially once the initial generation of MSN users grew older, the new '80, '85 and post-90s generation did not pay attention to MSN. Lacking attention and promotion, it was only a matter of time before MSN's reduced presence led to it being defeated entirely.

The second reason for their failure was the fact that there were a number of missteps in MSN's business model. After entering China, MSN had tried to open channels and promote themselves online, but the results left both advertisers and users feeling unsatisfied. In contrast, QQ's hierarchy and strategies, with platforms like QCoins and QQSpace, catered to the needs of younger users, thus allowing their base to expand.

Thirdly, the functionality of MSN's products was lacking. Although MSN shared more or less the same capabilities as QQ, it had been largely unreactive and blind towards trends on social networks and mobile internet. Users found its single chat function increasingly tedious and its active users began to decline. Advertisers dropped away accordingly and precipitated a loss of revenue. Eventually, the cycle proved unsustainable. In addition, just as IM software was being replaced by video chat, Microsoft remained static and unchanging, not paying attention to these new developments.

Worse still, from the point of view of bundling software, MSN exceeded QQ. After 2006, MSN bundled its browser, email and blogging tools into a package called Windows Live, which meant users were unwittingly installing all sorts of programs they did not want. The backlash, combined with regular web connection failures, caused MSN to fall in stature. The 2007 worm virus and other incidents further turned the program into an object of derision.

What was the effect of MSN's failure on people? The first was a lesson: innovation is king.

In an era of constant innovation, not only did products need to be constantly retooled to meet users' needs, but thinking itself needed to be 'short, frequent and fast' if it was to result in products with a competitive edge. By contrast, the alternative to MSN, Skype, had for some time occupied a number-one position in the global market, its path to success resting on how it allowed the computer to replace landline and mobile calls without bundling in unnecessary products or advertising that would turn users away.

The second lesson? One needs a clear business strategy. When it came to IM software, market share was a key factor in determining victory or defeat – it was the basic lifeline, regardless of business model. MSN's market share in China had never been able to exceed that of QQ, in part because Microsoft consistently disregarded the fact that there was no free version of its product.

Although MSN had targeted the business crowd, within nearly ten years it had been replaced by Tencent. Especially after entering the era of mobile internet, IM software and wireless client integration had effectively shrunk the space in which MSN worked, making the company that had once vowed to defeat QQ entirely obsolete.

THE ENCLOSURE
MOVEMENT

IF ONE IS NOT GIVEN HIGH VALUE, IT IS BECAUSE NONE YET EXISTS

In the emerging era of the internet, portal sites were always favoured by entrepreneurs, because, at that time, they were attractive to users. After a time of competing claims and staking of territory, Sina, Sohu and NetEase emerged as the three major web portals.

Most companies could not compete with these giants. But for Ma, having a portal was an essential step – he wanted to take part of the share claimed by the three titans in this area.

To some degree, it could be said that portals provide the sole means of acquiring diverse profits in the internet market. They can combine gaming, news, and advertising, all of which can then form a generous source of income for the website. With so many users, Ma could not pass up the opportunity. Surely to do otherwise would mean wasting the potential of all the users at hand? Thus, as part of QQ's ten year plan, he set out a goal of creating room for portals that would provide for casual and large-scale networking, e-commerce, and other value-added services.

As Ma conceived it, the portal would give Tencent a cross-connected business outlet to maximize QQ's cohesion. It would create a much larger platform with which to integrate resources and allow QQ to expand their services.

On 23 November 2003, Ma officially launched Tencent as an entertainment website combining news, fashion, entertainment, games, sports and chat, in addition to other areas. On 21 November, Tencent announced that its website had been involved in the rapidly growing gateway website market, a market which had been monopolized by Nasdaq-listed companies.

In fact, there were small differences between the portal Ma had created and traditional portals. Due to the fact that Ma's was entertainment-based, it could not avoid being interactive, unlike traditional search engines, which were more passive.

In an age of extensive portals, the internet knew only one harsh reality: there was no second place; the only available space was for a winner. There could be no harmonious 'blooming of a hundred flowers'. If one company pushed forward, another would have to exit. Industry experts pointed out that Tencent's road would inevitably be long and tortuous. Sina, Sohu and NetEase enjoyed the advantage of incumbency. They could frustrate newcomers. A newcomer, if they did not find some new method, would struggle in taking their established resources.

In fact, according to commentators, Ma was already aware of this, but had to persevere in his venture, lest the portal became a laughing stock. To this end, Ma stated confidently: "With our huge user base, Tencent is confident that QQ.com will reach the top three in three years."

Although many cast doubt on Ma's comment, it was not hard to recall, looking at the development of China's internet, that change was not the result of purely technical factors, but also material limits. Ma's desires were not underpinned by empty words, but by strategies that would evolve with the passage of time and became increasingly dangerous to the top three players.

DESKTOP PORTAL WIZARD

How far could Tencent go? Ma had built the network into an entertainment portal for younger people, and was determined to make it China's first fashion and entertainment portal. Meanwhile, he also pursued the development of wireless services to promote the films on the site, as well as news broadcasts, music-on-demand and e-commerce applications. Tencent's advantage lay in the support of its large user base, and its ability to style itself as *the* website for young people.

Throughout the years, Ma had pursued a business strategy of 'study + differentiation'. He would imitate peers or predecessors, but after each simulation, he would create something distinct and different. This was how QQ and its various offshoots were born. In this way, even if he was not at the forefront of innovation, he was always at the vanguard in terms of achievement, something his peers had to admire.

In order to increase the site's popularity, Ma launched a series of campaigns, such as a 2003 'Become a Star!' event with Motorola, which brought in a huge surge of new users.

With promotional activities in full swing, Ma introduced a new product: Tencent's mini home page. The mini home page allowed users to filter news into a digest of topics that interested them. Every time a user logged into QQ, the mini home page would appear. Ma also designed news popups to broadcast breaking news and a 'global connections' service, which assigned numbers to major events and topics. Users could then use these to follow the latest developments. The innovation created a 'blue ocean market' of new users outside the big three competitors.

With Tencent's star rising, the big three portals responded with their own software. But it was in vain – QQ now had nearly 600 million registered users.

From the end of 2003, in just three months, Tencent entered the top ten of portal rankings. By March 2006, it was second only to Sina – and third after Sina and Sohu in website hits. In April 2006, it was ranked above Sina and Sohu. By June of the same year, it was second only to Baidu, the Chinese equivalent of Google. It enjoyed daily traffic of 400 million users.

Despite its status, Ma knew he still needed time to accumulate the strength necessary to overwhelm the big three. They occupied a special place in the hearts of most netizens. Many people, when they first ventured onto the internet, had used these websites, and effort alone could not necessarily overcome the strength of that initial exposure and acculturation.

The 2005 China Fashion Ceremony, held in Shanghai, saw Tencent replacing Sina and TOM as the sole partner. Their portal was ranked eighth in the world, giving Ma confidence that he could lead them into a new stage of development: creating a desktop portal.

This portal was actually the biggest difference between Tencent and the other three big sites. It allowed them to instantly transmit updates to a user's computer desktop, unlike the other portals.

Tencent's mode of transmission focused on being interactive, community-based, aggregated and personalized. Tencent was leading a revolution, whose face could be seen in three aspects:

Firstly, it provided a new model for community users and an overall business layout.

The mini home page, for example, was a bold breakthrough in communication, combining instant messaging and advertising. With the portal's success, other companies, such as Microsoft's internet Explorer and MSN, scrambled to claim their own space, but they did not have the advantage of Tencent's early moves.

The second strength came in Tencent's employment of grassroots entertainment. Tencent's news perspectives came from exploring and investigating the levels they reported on, which were often issues of public concern. Sina, Sohu and NetEase took a different route, relatively elitist in comparison to Tencent's grassroots portal. Ma was basing his business upon the community who engaged with it, trying to provide users with information tailored to them, while combining communication with entertainment and business. Making users feel involved was key to satisfying them. QQ's news wires and new content-based quizzes helped Tencent create a platform that genuinely involved users. Ma's Tencent network represented a subversion of traditional news operations, promoting more extensive exchange and interactions between people.

In March 2006, the company formed a network with a Chongqing business newspaper. Within three months it had more than 1 million views, becoming the head of Chongqing's local online portals.

Why did Ma look into creating a regional portal? In an era of increasing internet usage, he saw that netizens in different areas needed more refined and specific services, and thus Chongqing was chosen as a guinea pig for new development.

Ma was able to source more abundant resources through local media, because regional portals had been ignored by many integrated portals and competition was not as fierce. With regional cooperation, Ma could establish dual interactive portals and media structures. Regional portals also needed an internet giant like Tencent to provide resources, while Tencent had a source of regional news.

The continuous injection of foreign capital gave regional portals a chance to expand; but Ma had already staked his territory and several provinces sought to cooperate with him. It was thus difficult for traditional portal giants, such as Sina, Sohu and NetEase to gain any advantage. Ma had divided their territories – perhaps even to the point where they would fall, like dominoes.

In 2014, Tencent's regional website had been running for eight years. After eight years of war and hard work, there had been a regional expansion of the portal to 12 major economic provinces, forming Tencent's 'comprehensive portal + urban life portal' matrix.

The company was at the summit in terms of its advertising market share, providing a rich source of profit for Ma. By focusing on economics and culture, Ma had emerged victorious in this new blue ocean market.

With regional portals included, Tencent had profits of over US$30 million. Ma had a strategy to target those users, through pop-ups that appeared on users' computers. The information these provided covered the user's work and life in the region. Through media impact and penetration, Ma had the last laugh.

CHAPTER

FIGHTING TO BECOME THE KING OF ONLINE BUSINESS

On 10 May 2003, the Alibaba Group's subsidiary, Taobao, was born. Unlike the B2B business model, Taobao was a cross between a B2C and C2C e-commerce platform.

If Alibaba was for businesses, and particularly SMEs, to build a platform for trading all over the world, Taobao was aimed at the individual, a platform for people-to-people trading. Many online companies were eyeing the market, looking to claim their own slice of the pie. On 12 June 2004, a very important moment in the history of the Chinese internet occurred: the West Lake Network Conference. More than 1,000 Chinese network operators gathered in Hangzhou at a conference hosted by the China e-Commerce Association and Alibaba. Many major brands, such as Walmart, LG, Samsung, Sears and GlaxoSmithKline made their Chinese procurements through Alibaba.

Clearly, e-commerce had become one of the internet's hottest businesses. Naturally, Ma could not miss such a golden opportunity. He had discovered that many Chinese users, being accustomed to physical shopping, would merely refer to a simple web page when shopping online, which often failed to show the real characteristics of the product and made it harder for the purchaser to trust it. He decided to put Tencent's speciality to work: strengthening online communications.

Ma's philosophy was that communication and mutual trust were crucial in e-commerce, and all the more important in the C2C industry. QQ was seen as just the right tool to compensate for the lack of communication in C2C transactions.

Ma even applied for a patent on his combination of QQ and e-commerce, whereby dialogue boxes, allowing buyers and sellers to communicate, would appear on-line. Of course, Ma realized many e-commerce sites had their own instant messaging software; however, QQ's were superior.

The next step was to consider how to bring buyers to-gether. This was an easy problem to resolve: QQ's huge pool of users was a large market in itself.

Though there were 400 million registered and over 170 million active users, this did not preclude making an ini-tial incursion into the C2C platform. Ma knew that e-com-merce was still in its initial stages, and it was simply a mat-ter of time before their scope could expand.

On 12 September 2005, Ma released his C2C platform: Paipai. Like Taobao and Alipay, it ensured the security of online transactions. The environment was challenging, giv-en that Taobao was fairly mature and well established at this time, and there was also eBay to contend with.

Initially, trials of Paipai were planned to see if it was ready to be transferred to an operational state. In order to give users a sense of intimacy, Ma sent a letter through Pai-pai. Since the 2002 fee controversy, Ma had become very cautious with users, and made every effort to ensure they were satisfied, and that there was a sense of openness and transparency in Tencent's plans.

PAIPAI FORMALLY LAUNCHED

On 13 March 2006, Paipai entered its operational phase. Relying on the support of 170 million active users, it had 9 million registered users after its official launch. Based on surveys, most users welcomed the chat function. Relevant data showed that 70% of the C2C market was already taken and that there seemed to be little space for expansion; but Ma felt that there was still potential to establish links with many users who remained unconnected.

Paipai's network architecture was very advanced: users could enter online shops, interact with avatars, see star ratings of sellers, and sellers could make buyers into VIP customers, who could then enjoy discount offers.

On 10 May 2006, Taobao – which had gained the advantage during its competition with eBay – started to charge sellers, by providing a competing fee-paying ranking service, Zhao Cai Jin Bao.

This service meant that all qualified Taobao goods could be presented at the highest positions on Taobao. After the promised three-year free period, this fee-paying value-added service was widely considered to be an effective means of charging sellers, and also proved the most significant reform of Taobao since its establishment.

However, sellers were angry about the policy. They believed it would see sellers' products being placed far towards the end of Baidu search results, leading to a turnover rate of nil.

The CEO of Taobao stated that the model was completely new to C2C, and that users would understand its benefits after using it. He used data to back up this claim: 20 days after its launch, 100,000 sellers had already taken part.

For many, though, the words were empty: those who did not participate in the bidding saw their businesses take a nosedive. By 30 May 2006, an online petition had attracted 39,326 signatures. If there was no response to their collective strike by 1 June, they would cease sales and withdraw their Paypal funds.

Ma could see that Taobao's initiative not only hurt sellers, but was also affecting buyers. He decided to use the opportunity to develop his own Paipai. Soon after, Paipai initiated a campaign called 'Home-Moving Ants' with the slogan, "heavy rain comes and the ants are moving". This seemed an apt motto since, at that time, ants were Taobao's mascot. Clearly, Ma intended to lure Taobao sellers to move to Paipai with the free slogan. In order to increase its publicity, this campaign was promoted throughout the QQ platform. Paipai even promised that it would accept sellers' prior credit records from third-party platforms and provide recommended positions for newly opened shops. It was a clear challenge to Taobao.

In order to attract more sellers to Paipai, Ma also introduced a policy of special incentives users could participate in, such as third-party transfers and shopper rewards.

On 6 June 2006, Paipai was officially launched, with users being able to utilize its services free of charge for three years. With more and more users online, sellers also wanted to find a prime position for selling their products, and Ma hoped that that the measures the company had installed would attract them.

According to reports, in the second quarter of 2006, China's C2C had a market size of ¥5.71 billion, showing a strong momentum of development and growth. From September 2005 to August 2006, Paipai grew rapidly, its registered users exceeding 2 million a year and online sales breaking the 4.5 million mark.

In facing Paipai's challenges and its direct provocation in the Zhao Cai Jin Bao event, Ma Yun was certainly not pleased. However, at this point, a rumour spread online: the prior protest of Taobao users was alleged to have been planned by Paipai.

On 30 May 2006, an anonymous article was published online, entitled "How Tencent attacked Taobao". The article claimed that Tencent and a PR firm signed an online forum PR agency agreement designed to denounce Taobao. The article was followed up with a survey asking people whether they believed that Ma had collaborated with someone to attack Taobao.

Ma issued a letter from his lawyers, requesting the immediate deletion of both articles. However, although the articles were removed from the direct listings, they were not completely deleted. On 6 June, a further article was published, called, "Tencent's 10 Deadly Sins".

The article was filled with personal attacks and name-calling. Seeing red, Ma took the company who published the articles to court, demanding an apology and ¥5 million in compensation.

On 21 June, the battle reached a climax. Ma pointed out that difficult innovations tended to rely on copying: all e-commerce companies were inclined to copy, and it was often impossible to say who had copied whom. Internal contradictions aside, on the one hand, Taobao was the one who had developed the principles, while Paipai followed them. If Taobao applied to patent its model, it could not be disputed that Ma's behaviour was an infringement. On the other hand, in the rapid development of the internet, no one could restrict or bind any one model. All any company could rely on was strong talk and persuasion.

In December 2006, Tencent filed a lawsuit against Taobao. The basis of the case was that Taobao was selling QQ coins cheaply. They believed this would never have happened without Tencent's cooperation with Taobao.

Prior to suing Taobao, Tencent had repeatedly reminded Taobao that their actions were in violation of Tencent's rights, only resorting to the law as a last safeguard for their rights and interests.

In fact, the spark that started the fire was a shop that had opened on Taobao's website. The shop had sold QQ dollars. When Tencent discovered this, they negotiated with Taobao, and Tencent hoped to be able to convince the business to stop the practice, or simply close their store. But Taobao ultimately took no real notice of Tencent's warning.

Thus Tenent took Taobao to court, claiming a violation of their property rights and copyright, and seeking to have the store's page deleted.

However, ingeniously, Taobao had taken legal action first, seeking legal validation from the court. From their point of view, the sale of QQ coins was an independent marketplace, and Tencent's actions were an unfair attempt to shut down competition. In other words, Taobao was merely a platform – what sellers did on that platform was an unrelated matter for which Taobao could not be held responsible.

Tencent was unwilling to settle so amicably, and stated that such a trading platform would be unworkable in the first place.

As the conflict continued, Shenzhen police shut down the account responsible for stealing QQ accounts and coins, much to the delight of Tencent.

Yet the situation remained unsettled. In a sense, Taobao could be considered a house in which rooms were rented – could it really be said that, just because some of the rooms in the household were not clean, they should be driven out? Absolutely not.

In addition, Taobao was unlikely to have its businesses 'filtered'. Tencent stated that Taobao should set up a filter for merchants intending to do business on Taobao. However, the cost of doing so was prohibitive and inconsistent with the internet's needs to be fast and varied. Taobao were determined not to comply.

Taobao saw what they provided as merely a personal trading platform and were passive in their approach to it. But with such an approach, the platform was flooded with those who played by their own rules and pursued their own interests.

COMPETING WITH SOCIAL NETWORKING SERVICES

By 2006, the concept of the internet was deeply rooted, and more companies were moving their focus to social networking services (SNS) and what they could bring to netizens. The US had become well known for their contribution to this emerging space, through the use of Facebook. Jack Ma, head of Taobao, could see the potential of this market and was active in developing a strategy for Taobao.

They were not alone. Alibaba were also investigating the advantages of this area, as Taobao actively attempted to seek out talent in SNS development.

If Jack Ma could build bridges between e-commerce and the SNS communities, Alibaba would have a problem on their hands. In terms of talent, there were only two companies at the time capable of creating something like Facebook: Tencent and Alibaba.

Pony Ma was also examining the potential of this area. On Weibo he expressed Tencent's interest, thus placing him in direct competition with Jack Ma.

On 1 September 2010, war ignited between Tencent and Taobao. On 31 August, Tencent initiated a comprehensive ban against Taobao's new search engine algorithms. Taobao, in turn, banned promoters with Tencent's QQ numbers. The intention was for Taobao to be able to promote their own instant messaging, while suppressing their rival.

For Jack Ma, the battle had already been won from the moment eBay could no longer compete with Taobao. By maintaining a localized service over the course of their development, they had managed to fend off both Paipai and eBay.

Compared with Alibaba, Tencent's product line was too long, making it hard for Ma to concentrate his energy on e-commerce. Perhaps this gave Taobao an indication of Paipai's future downfall.

Over time, the competition between Paipai and Taobao eventually became one-sided: Taobao gradually overcame. Whether because of the size of Tencent's product range or Jack Ma's skills, Paipai never had a chance to defeat Taobao. In 2007, Taobao was no longer a simple auction site, but the largest of Asia's online retailers.

Although Ma enjoyed nothing comparable to such e-commerce success and Paipai could not compete with Taobao, he managed to recommend it to the Jingdong group in the B2C market.

As part of Jingdong's strategic cooperation agreement with Tencent, Tencent agreed to provide Jingdong access to WeChat and QQ customers to help them find new markets in electronics; they also agreed to cooperate in online payments, thus enhancing users' online experience.

Although the act of passing Paipai on to Jingdong may have appeared as though Pony Ma had lost to Jack Ma, Tencent's 15% stake in Jingdong meant that they were able to combine advantages. They were able to merge Jingdong's distribution channels with Tencent's mobile connectivity and user base.

So how had Paipai failed where Tencent had succeeded? First, there was no causal connection between having a large number of users and some degree of success in C2C.

Once Ma had attracted hundreds of millions of users, it was necessary to maintain user wishes and the familiar relationships and interests they had cultivated online. In order to maintain this familiarity, it was not enough to simply transplant everything to a more transparently commercial context, as this would weaken the hold they had on users.

Secondly, the advantages of QQ's community model were difficult to translate into business advantages.

As an IM software, QQ was quite successful, creating a huge community into which most of China's internet users could be absorbed. However, being a community, it was mainly seen as meeting interpersonal needs rather than consumer ones. By contrast, Taobao had gathered together a growing number of businesses, which in turn attracted more and more buyers.

Thirdly, there was not enough attention paid to user's needs. Given QQ's ability to connect people, and the ability of Alipay and Taobao to meet consumer needs, Paipai had few distinct advantages through which to distinguish itself, and thus became viewed by most users as largely redundant. Much to Ma's regret, Paipai was never able to compete with Taobao.

In 2014, Alibaba and Tencent released two new pieces of software. Industry saw the confrontation as representative of a battle for either side to prove their strength. Tencent, for its part, was moving into restaurant reviews and other such areas of IM software, some of them not dissimilar to Uber.

The first shots were fired in earnest on 10 January 2014. On that day, Didi announced that it would provide taxi drivers with a share of earnings as a kind of subsidy. After the news broke, many taxi drivers downloaded the app, as did users themselves.

As of 30 June 2014, Didi had a 45% share of the market of over 178 cities. Alibaba's service claimed the rest of the market over 306 cities. In early August, the two services still paid symbolic awards to taxi drivers, but far less than they had in the first half of the year. Eventually the subsidy dropped to ¥2, before ceasing altogether.

Each service was influenced by the culture of its parent company. Kuaide, being owned by Alibaba, was able to find understanding partners in the area of e-commerce and to win user loyalty. Tencent meanwhile had a strong advantage in its social networking platform and viral promotion strategies.

The next stage in the war came when both sides began competing for limousine services. Beginning in Beijing, the service spread across the country, while some cities saw their local government transportation departments calling for a stop to the services.

Taxi management policy lagged behind changes in technology, causing some to wonder if technology would determine the trends that a market economy would have to follow, or even lead to reform of the entire taxi industry.

CHAPTER

SEARCH ENGINES BECOME PREVALENT

COMPETITIVE RANKINGS PROVE LUCRATIVE

Internet search engines had come to be viewed as virtual pots of gold: a source of potentially endless money. Each business area had its fixed profit point for search engines, and thus one of the main sources of income was keyword advertising. Companies would pay according to their ranking, and thus a major strategy was to buy keywords that would rank them higher in search engine results.

In China, Baidu was the major search engine. Enterprises looking to increase their visibility on the search engine were a huge source of profit for the company. In November 2008, news was released saying that some businesses were advertising on Baidu without being properly reviewed. Other media outlets published similar reports, saying that Baidu's bid-ranking system was a source of vicious and unrestrained competition.

Given Baidu's exposure, some 1 billion people would have been exposed to the news. Baidu's stock plunged, falling by 38% over just three trading days.

However, Baidu's problem was not simply the loss of money but, more critically, the loss of a more intangible value – its brand image. Yet the controversy did prompt a re-evaluation of their business ethics, as well as reveal a hidden source of search engine revenue, and so Baidu moved its focus on to pastures new.

In 2005, with the rise of the search engine market in China, Ma began to intensify his focus upon this area. He was keenly aware that, as long as portal sites could only provide information, users were mere passive recipients, unable to actively interact with the information they collected. This was a gap in the portal concept.

On 4 February 2005, Ma and Google reached a strategic cooperation plan to help Tencent expand its search engine strength. In exchange for Google providing web search services, Tencent would help Google with internet advertising and search engine technology.

After this mutual collaboration, Ma began the next stage of his plan, ensuring users would receive information customized to their needs and interests. On 2 March 2006, Tencent released its search engine. Compared with other well-known search engines, its focus was on meeting user – and in particular young people's – needs.

The search engine included options for pictures, news, music, and other forums, as well as connection with QQ via the same login.

At first, Baidu seemed to take this development lightly, appearing unconcerned. However, given the tendency of search engines to aim for complete coverage of all areas of the internet as their ultimate purpose, a collision seemed inevitable.

In June 2005, Sina attempted to break into the search engine market with software that combined the input of various companies' content and resources, but after two years it was clear that it had very little chance of competing with the dominating power of Baidu and Google.

By 2007, with Google's China localization strategy having proven unsuccessful, and Sina having failed to find success, Sina and Google announced a plan to cooperate with each other.

One reason for Google's loss to Baidu was that Baidu held a 'business licence, while Google did not. Google and Sina's cooperation, despite great fanfare, proved to simply be Sina using Google's search engine. At this point, Zhang Chaoyang, head of Sohu, emerged. In 1998, he introduced Sohu, and in 2000, the company listed on NASDAQ.

In 2004, Sohu introduced a search engine, placing him in direct competition with Baidu. Its name was said to come from the words *sou* and *gou*, which, in Chinese, means 'search dog'. Two years later, Baidu remained top dog, having lost nothing to Sohu.

Ma, for his part, had still not found a way to compete with Baidu in the search engine market. But he still had confidence in Tencent's large number of users, and continued to search for opportunities in the area.

By 2014, Baidu already had over 1 billion registered users and daily page views of over 2.7 billion. Its younger user base was an important part of its predominance. Its message boards also helped these users, both to pursue individuality and to find like-minded people. These message boards were a formative part of the fan culture that developed online in China. They also gave it the popularity necessary for developing it into China's main search engine.

Baidu's advantage over the QQ group was that it created a sense of community and a stronger sense of belonging, whereas QQ was mostly simply a messaging tool. Ma was inspired to try and integrate the experience of search engines with Tencent's existing products, in order to create a personal, community-based, intelligent, agile product.

Following Google's exit from China, Tencent's search engine had one less competitor to contend with, and with many former Google staff coming over to Tencent, their chances of rising were further enhanced.

Still, integrating Google's advanced technology and experience into the company and search engine would take time. However, the new influx of talent provided Ma with many new directions to explore if he wanted to overtake Baidu.

10 CHAPTER

THE PENGUIN
WANTS TO PLAY

FIRST ATTEMPTS AT ONLINE GAMING

In 2006, a US securities firm released a report that predicted gaming would account for 50% of all game industry revenue over the next five years.

In February 2006, QQ games broke the 2 million mark of simultaneous online users. After eight years of development, China's online game market had established the record for the most simultaneous online users.

Ma still had competition, though, and developed a plan for the company that saw them, in May 2003, developing software to meet Chinese gamers' increasingly sophisticated needs by having 3D gaming replace 2D software. Alongside a Korean developer, they produced a game called Return Triumphant.

On 7 July 2004, at a Chinese international software exposition, it was stated that, "Tencent, after listing on the stockmarket with US$20 million, has set its sights on the gaming market." Ma then created several teams, in order to realize his goal as quickly as possible.

It was within this context and sense of expectancy that Return Triumphant was released.

In all respects, the game was superior to its 2D forebears. The fact it could be used regardless of the quality of the user's computer helped its fame to spread. Ease of payment, through mobile or Q coins, also proved advantageous.

Although it had no real competition, some problems did emerge, such as servers being unable to cope with the popularity and size of the game. Nonetheless, if these problems could be overcome, the success of the other aspects of Tencent's business boded well for the future.

HEROES

Pony Ma's first attempt at being licensed to operate online games proved a huge failure, and no doubt presented a relatively major setback to Tencent, as it had just entered the online game market. Nevertheless, Ma quickly learned his lesson and made a significant decision: on the one hand, Tencent should make full use of its rich user base to strengthen its gaming platform; on the other hand, in order to gain more experience, Tencent should split its operations into different zones. From this point forward, Ma was no longer satisfied with having copycat games, or simply being licensed to operate games. He wanted to develop original games.

Soon thereafter, Tencent targeted the then online game magnate, Shanda Game, as its presumptive rival.

When Tencent released QQ Chess and Cards, Shanda had just acquired the Bianfeng Games Platform. However, within just one year, QQ Chess and Cards presented itself as superior to chess and card games platforms like Ourgame and Bianfeng, making it the king of all similar platforms. More importantly, Tencent had broken the curse of chess and card games not being profitable, demonstrating the remarkable power of the little penguin to the Chinese online game market.

Although Tencent did not have a great deal of experience operating online games, it was very experienced in commercial promotion to users. Tencent had cooperated successively with companies like Huaxia Beijing and Dreakworks Chengdu to operate several games, including Huaxia and Xiayidao.

In 2004, Tencent advanced its new online game, QQ Tang, which quickly gained the favour of users. Even though QQ Tang was considered by some to be a copycat of Shenda's Paopao Tang, the online game had over a few million players every day.

Ma built upon the momentum of QQ Tang's success. He continued to make copycats while maintaining a small scale research, development and licensed online games business: QQ Battle Platform was a copycat of Haofang Battle Platform; QQ Three Kingdoms was a copycat of The Adventure Island; QQ Racing Cars copied Crazyracing Kartrider, and QQ Dancing copied Audition Online.

No matter how many people held a grudge against Ma's strategy of copying other companies, they could not deny the fact that those much-criticized games were also proof that Tencent was not afraid of competing with its rivals with similar products. The games that had been copied by Tencent showed a resulting decrease in sales.

Subsequently, in 2005, Ma invested ¥30 million into the development of a large online game, QQ Fantasy, over two years. As an online-community game, QQ Fantasy represented a huge step on the part of Tencent towards its plans for establishing an online community.

While accumulating its experience in operating casual online games, Tencent began to develop larger online games. Eventually it promoted its signature games, Journey to Fairyland and Dungeon Fighter Online (the latter developed by a Korean company). Ma had given the two lines of products a great deal of consideration, and the two games were totally different in nature and content: one made in China while the other was made in Korea, one in 3D while the other was 2D.

In relation to the controversies of the online games, Ma had his own opinion: "Any service must be provided to its users in an orderly and appropriate way. Otherwise, no matter whether the game is for casual entertainment or education, if it costs too much time for the users, it will be inappropriate."

In order to further promote the positive image of QQ Fantasy, Ma cooperated with the Wahaha Group. Through this cooperation, Ma learned that, after a few years' development, the Chinese online gaming market was heading towards a more specialized direction, and would become more mature and stable as domestic online game developers strengthened their research and development capacity. For Tencent, there were still many unexplored opportunities ahead.

THE INCREASED UNPREDICTABILITY OF THE MOBILE GAMING AGE

On 13 August 2014, Tencent published its Q2 financial report. Total revenue stood at ¥19.746 billion. Online gaming revenue had reached ¥11.081 billion, a significant increase. And the mobile version of QQ and mobile games attached to WeChat had reached ¥3 billion, 30% of total online gaming revenue. Moreover, Tencent had made remarkable progress in the area of online game patenting. As of 20 November 2014, Tencent had acquired 64 patents in online games, while Huawei, ranked second in the market, had 41 patents. In recent years, Tencent has held a leading position in terms of patent applications. This represents but one demonstration of Ma's continuous creativity in the online gaming area.

Currently, Tencent Games has already become one of the biggest domestic online gaming social communities. Under the open internet strategy advanced by Ma, Tencent

Games covers five categories, including casual gaming platforms, huge online games, middle-scale casual games, table games and battle platforms.

At present, the contribution made by PC games like The Viral Factors, Blade and Soul, and League of Legends are the primary sources of income. Moreover, Tencent has also created Dungeon Fighter Online, LOL, and Crossfire, which are the top three games in terms of global online profitability. Even so, the rapid development of mobile games has already severely impacted PC gaming. Since this is a common problem in the industry, it is certainly not a challenge that could be resolved by Ma alone.

Currently, Ma has not officially ventured into the mobile chess and card games market. What he has thus far done is simply transplant the existing PC chess and cards games to mobile phones, relying primarily on the large amount of users and the popularity accumulated over the past few years. But once Tencent had determined to aggregate these games, it definitely created a more attractive mobile chess and card gaming platform, which could not easily be matched by other companies.

As a tycoon in the PC chess and card gaming area, Tencent's monopoly position had been challenged by mobile gaming. Nevertheless, as stated by Tencent, in the future, its mobile game business would provide a source of stable income. Tencent would also speed up the development of its new mobile games, as well as invite third parties to collaborate on its projects.

Although WeChat already had a considerable competitive edge, combined with the advantage of a few hundred million users in the mobile market, the mobile games industry was still restricted by the profit-generating model of conventional games. Compared to conventional PC games and mobile game apps, the active users of Tencent WeChat were mostly urban or in the middle or higher classes. For users of this type, the major motivation for logging onto WeChat was to enjoy some relaxation and casual entertainment, not to consume virtual commercial goods. From this perspective, the profitability of mobile games was still somewhat restricted.

Tencent's mobile terminals had already absorbed all of the Chinese internet users. With the promotion of Tencent, many non-players had gradually been transformed into casual players, while many of these casual players had been converted into frequent players. However, there were some restraints in terms of Tencent's data volume transmission and the users' data input capacity. Tencent was experiencing a bottleneck period in the operation of its online social community platform. Hence, Tencent had created Yingyong Bao as another channel of development. However, since Yingyong Bao was currently relying on WeChat and QQ Mobile to direct user traffic, some of the Tencent mobile games could only be downloaded through Yingyong Bao, and this had exerted some pressure on the further development of Yingyong Bao. If the operators failed to maintain the business properly, or adopted an unreasonable business strategy, it would lead to a series of negative repercussions.

In the age of mobile games, whether Tencent was able to become a leading figure with the success of WeChat was dependent upon how Ma and his penguin army would devise and enforce their strategies.

"ENEMY OF THE STATE" AS A MAJOR PLAYER, OR, COPYING IS THE MOTHER OF INNOVATION

It seems that Tencent is the only example of an enemy of the state in the Chinese internet market. It is also the only enterprise that can cover almost all online services and products. Hence, people have transformed the famous line of Tang Jun, "My success can be copied", into "My copying can make success", in order to mock Tencent. Actually, this is exactly the core value of the penguin empire.

Copying and innovation have always been the trump cards of Ma, and this collaborative approach represents his business strategy of 'standing on the shoulders of giants'. Ma knows very well that it is very hard, perhaps even dangerous, to be a pioneer in the Chinese market, since it lacks the innovation and creativity of foreign markets. Therefore, he has been determined to choose the path of 'copying + innovation'.

Although many people thought that this strategy demonstrated Ma's exploitation of the innovators, apart from the QICQ domain name case, Tencent had barely encountered any major lawsuits.

The real reason for Tencent's ability to avoid being sued, even while it was making copycats of other companies' products, was that the core technologies did not belong to China from the start. For example, the famous Alipay and some other video technologies were introduced from abroad. Therefore, many of the companies copied by Ma were themselves copiers. They were all, like Ma, borrowing foreign business models.

Ma was quite successful in terms of providing a satisfying user experience. 'People first,' had always been his creed, so that, no matter what he copied, he would do no worse than his competitors. It is exactly for this reason that many people within the industry thought that, within the Chinese internet market, there was no such thing as 100% innovation – no matter whether one was referring to tycoons or smaller enterprises. Assuming the idea of making copies is utilized as a standard, nobody can be called innocent. Thus, what people really feel to be taboo is not so much the act of copying itself, but copying without innovation.

Let us examine the innovations of QQ. For instance, services such as QQ Vip, and QQ's Blue Diamonds and Red Diamonds were not copied by Ma from elsewhere, but rather were original creations. Through such innovation, Tencent was able to expand and maintain its user base. The value-added services developed by Ma also helped Tencent's bottom line. With the support of a huge number of users, Ma was able to continue to copy and perfect every imitation, according to users' varying demands.

UNDERSTAND USER DEMANDS

Undoubtedly, the reason that Tencent could enjoy such a massive market was because it had a huge and stable user group. This user group had been acquired by knowing and understanding the psychological needs of users.

Many users felt that the file transmission speed of QQ was fairly quick – this kind of feedback from users ensured the advantage of Tencent. Ma would pay attention to the feedback and ensure their advantages were further improved and perfected, thereby adding value to their brand name.

Ma believed that the hardest part of designing products was prioritization and ordering. Therefore, he would not form judgments about products based simply on volume reports completed by employees, since these types of reports usually involved lots of subjectivity. Ma always expected that the product managers would explore the potential problems and ramifications when they first started to devise a product, and therefore put a great deal of attention into the product itself. With this type of focused attention, the result would usually be successful and effective.

Ma placed much emphasis on the core function of a product, whether that be to save time, solve problems or promote efficiency. Ma's requirements for the Tencent product managers were to: be capable; be confident; pay attention to the core function of the product; and have a passion for pushing things forward.

In Ma's opinion, the user experience required technological breakthroughs. In order to achieve this, Ma required effort be invested into exploration of the hard indicators of the product. At the stage of design and development, the designers had to consider how the outside world would compare the Tencent product with similar products.

Ma actually required Tencent to develop the core capacities of the product to its extreme. Once this was achieved, it was harder for potential rivals to catch up, and Tencent could exert its competitive edge.

Ma still considered the product managers to be a kind of spearhead, as all product upgrades required the cooperation of the managers. Because of this, Ma allowed more experienced senior technological researchers to be promoted to product manager positions. Ma felt that a good product needed to be controlled by someone capable and experienced. Otherwise, if a manager were unqualified, he or she would always need others' help, and the final result could potentially be unsatisfactory.

No matter what the product, feedback and comments were critical. This valuable reponse usually came from senior users and opinion leaders. In the past, Ma's strategy had been to emphasize the less senior and less advanced users' demands. However, as Tencent developed, he had become increasingly aware of the demands of more senior and advanced users.

This raised a crucial question:, how could he attract more senior and advanced users? Ma believed that this only became a meaningful problem once the fundamental functions had been fully explored. For example, he felt that, until a Tencent product had gained user comments, they should not abuse the platform's functions. The product managers therefore had first to pay attention to the parts that would satisfy user demands. Without these, users would only give negative feedback. On the other hand, given the increased number of users, existing users could help by promoting the products that they were satisfied with. Therefore, Ma had been quite discreet and cautious in terms of development and promotion. He put a great deal of consideration into every update. It was this constructive attitude that helped him to promote his products. Ma was aware that, if the reputation of the product were ruined, it would be extremely difficult to recover the loss.

Ma kept updating Tencent's products. At the same time, he gained a rich experience in controlling the functions of the various products. Once the core function of a product was completed, other frequently used functions were gradually completed. The designers had to carefully consider every one of the problems. One of the most frequently encountered problems was: when a function could bring, for example, 10% of the users some positive effect, would it then have a negative effect for the remaining users? It often required a great deal of effort to resolve the inner conflicts of the products themselves. It was crucial for the managers to learn how to provide different solutions for a variety of situations. In other words, having more functions was not a major determiner of success; a far more accurate measure was that of users' overall satisfaction.

Prioritizing the users' experience helped to target their various demands precisely, providing the company with new pathways and prospects. It was Ma's 'user first' creed that allowed Tencent to survive and thrive in such a fiercely competitive market.

GROWING ADDICTION TO TENCENT PRODUCTS

Nowadays, many Tencent users have become 'addicted' to Tencent products: this is not only true of QQ, but also of WeChat and QQ games, among others. With the wide use of smartphones and the development of the internet, Tencent products have a huge appeal and many users have developed a heavy reliance on them.

What Ma had been thinking about was how to maintain this attractiveness. In other words, how to keep users addicted.

The first aim is always to maintain the products' simplicity. In the age of the internet and wireless applications, simplicity is a vital principle for designers. Ma has never been in favour of complicated buttons that affect the users' experience; instead, he has always strived to simplify the operation of his products, no matter the purpose of the product or the type of intended users. Sometimes, one of his prerequisites has been that children should be able to operate the product freely.

The second vital step towards maintaining product attractiveness has been designing products that allow users to multitask. Whenever Ma designed an app, he would first consider the user's location and the time at which they would be using the product. Often, if a product required too much attention or time to operate, it would adversely affect the user's experience.

Take QQ as an example: its operation is quite simple, allowing people to chat while surfing the internet. Crucially it does not occupy too much of user's concentration, especially since the introduction of the combination of different chat windows. Users are able to chat with many different people while saving screen space. All these updates are intended to promote ease of usage, while demanding minimal amounts of concentration from the user.

The third factor influencing product attractiveness has been the development of products that allow the users to develop a feeling of control. On the internet, giving users a sense of autonomy and freedom in decision-making are key principles for successful products.

Fourthly, Ma realized that micro-innovation stimulates users. Given the huge number of internet products available, creating an addiction among users requires promoting positive effects, which will, in turn facilitate a positive emotional reaction. Furthermore, Ma noted that as users grow tired of the software, they will develop a resistance against it and may not wish to use it again. Therefore, in order to maintain the user's interest, Ma always tried to find means of gradually build up stimulation among users, progressively propelling them toward increased usage.

The fifth important factor involved paying attention to the ways in which users absorb information through conscious and sub-conscious means. In order to develop an addiction, Ma always used a great deal of creativity to encourage users to employ their products repeatedly. In the process, he would transmit information to the users through both their conscious and sub-conscious mind, while simultaneously maintaining a positive interaction between the users and the software.

The sixth crucial strategy constituted ensuring that users engage with the product repeatedly. Tencent has created lots of QQ games relating to wealth, which allow users to repeat a number of simple acts and gain positive feedback as a result. For instance, when playing some Mahjong card games, users could gain virtual rewards. These rewards would cause dopamine releases in the user, making the user feel positively towards the product. Once users became accustomed to this habit, their brains would release more dopamine and continually encourage the users to keep engaging with the product.

The seventh factor was making the users feel 'cool'. No matter whether in the real or in virtual world, every individual wants to feel superior and to feel they are making progress, especially when compared with others. Ma had observed this common mentality, so during the process of development, he put a great deal of consideration into this aspect. For example, QQ Vip can be upgraded with yellow diamonds. In social software QQ and WeChat, the 'like' function provides another way to highlight one's popularity, while gaining the attention of friends. Ma theorized that the need to show off and gain recognition would encourage users to employ the product repeatedly, as well as providing more profit-generating channels.

Lastly, it was important to compliment users continually. In the virtual world, Ma valued exaggerating positive feedback. Adopting this measure, users would fall into a loop of using Tencent products in order to gain a sense of appreciation and success.

In the current competitive software market, only those who can cultivate the addiction of their users can profit. Through the employment of these various effective strategies, Ma's team continue to be successful in this way.

11
CHAPTER

A NEW STRATEGY DRIVES THE COMPETITION CRAZY

WITH 800 MILLION USERS, THERE IS NOTHING TO FEAR

On 16 May 2007, Tencent published its Q1 financial report for 2007: as of 31 March 2007, QQ had 597.9 million registered users, with 253.7 million of them active. The biggest number of users online simultaneously was 28.5 million.

In 2011, Tencent organized a massive high-level conference. During the course of this conference, Tencent and all of its third-party partners discussed their open strategy. The commercial purpose of the discussion was that Ma intended to share the fruits of Tencent QQ with everyone.

During the 3Q War in 2011, Ma had made a tough decision: to allow 360 software users to use QQ. It was this seemingly insignificant decision that had changed the fate of Tencent fundamentally; indeed, it had arguably even transformed the status of the Chinese internet industry and its hundreds of millions of users.

Some days after the 3Q War, on 17 November 2010, Ma attended the 12th Entrepreneur Summit of China. Here, he stated that, "While the internet has been affecting people's lives profoundly, it provides many opportunities. Openness and sharing have formed the primary trends in our industry. In the future, Tencent will attempt to implement more elements of openness and sharing into the industry. And we will further promote open platforms pragmatically, cooperating with app developers and independent developers to collaboratively facilitate the development of China's internet."

Ma's open strategy meant users would be able to enjoy the more humane and vibrant online life provided by Tencent through the means of software such as Q+, which allowed third-party applications to use QQ as a stage to provide services directly to more than 600 million QQ users.

The true intention of such an idea was to form a massive group of users: a more open and intelligent community integrated into the entire online world, with each part connected organically. From Q+ it could be seen that one of Ma's important corporate visions was to make QQ not only the core business of Tencent, but also the core of an entire internet industry chain. It would become the preliminary impetus for all kinds of online activities for Chinese users.

THE RALLYING POWER OF MA'S Q+

In 2014, the international social marketing agency We Are Social conducted a survey and published a ranking of the major global internet social platforms. Among the five largest social networking service providers, Tencent QQ, QQ Space and WeChat made the list. The reports stated that, in 2014, the total number of global internet users exceeded 3 billion. Among them, the active monthly users of Facebook numbered 1.35 billion, close to the total population of China. The second and third places belonged to QQ and QQ Space, its total registered users numbering 829 million, with 645 million active monthly users. The fifth entry was the instant messaging mobile application WeChat. Its active monthly users numbered 438 million.

Over the past few years, WeChat's development in the Chinese market has exceeded that of QQ and QQ Space. The phenomenon has attracted wide attention from the West. The reason behind this is closely connected to the contribution and effect of QQ, since at least half of WeChat's users are also QQ users.

From 600 million to 829 million; the huge number of users again demonstrated Tencent's power. With such a massive user group, no matter what kind of software was created by Tencent, the product would always be used by hundreds of millions of people.

USE THREE HANDS TO DIG FOR GOLD

In 2012, Ma reorganized the mobile department of Tencent to make it more suitable for the new mobile internet age. In order to enhance the appeal of the mobile business, he adopted the strategy of 'using two hands to dig for gold'.

On the one hand was the mobile internet business. This group attempted to integrate the wireless department and the PC department of Tencent into one business chain, to help facilitate the development of Tencent's mobile internet. On the other hand was WeChat, a new product for a new age, which could respond to the user's experience and demands. It is likely WeChat will continue to play an important part in the future development strategies of Tencent.

Of course, for Ma, both hands could hit competitors concurrently, but not without some inevitable drawbacks. For instance, the design for the mobile business was not sufficient to advance Ma's grand strategy, and could only generate some short-term revenue. However, because it had originated from the relevant parts of the PC business, many conventional departments had become its power source. Ironically, the mobile internet business had partly replaced the PC business, causing inevitable conflict between the different departments.

Furthermore, because there were some related investments between WeChat and the mobile internet business, their development would occupy the resources of other departments. In this way, Ma's two hands sometimes intertwined and tangled together.

Following the improvement of Tencent's mobile internet products and Ma's understanding of the mobile internet business, the habitual two-hand strategy was no longer capable of satisfying their demands, so another 'invisible hand' had to be added. This invisible hand was the mobile interactive entertainment business which absorbed the mobile QQ business and mobile games. After the reorganization, the mobile department was no longer a 'vampire', but a blood generator. Ma encouraged other departments to invest funds and energy into the mobile department as well.

However, from the outside, Ma's arrangement might have appeared somewhat ambivalent, suggesting Tencent had not made WeChat into a driver so much as a long-running experiment. In fact, Tencent's three-hand strategy differed greatly from the previous two-hands approach.

This was due to the fact that the mobile internet business did not carry a heavy pressure to profit in the short term, making WeChat more important; furthermore, the profit-generating businesses, such as mobile QQ and mobile games, returned to the PC department after the reorganization, further increasing its commercial value and the company revenue, while decreasing the commercial pressure on WeChat.

In 2014, Tencent held the Tencent Mobile Open Strategy Conference. The parties present revealed their plans for future strategy and products. As one of the internet tycoons, Tencent did not fail to meet expectations, revealing some details of their mobile business strategy.

During this conference, Tencent promoted Yingyong Bao as a major product. This new product had potential for broad development in the future. What determined its value was the new Tencent strategy, aimed at 'digging deeply into the social genes'. This demonstrated Ma's attempt at finding new pathways to more personalized products and resources. Users and developers could realize their best interests, and allow Tencent to differentiate itself from its competitors in the future market.

Yingyong Bao was different from traditional application distribution. It was more personalized and the upgraded 4.0 version was able to analyse the user's personal preferences, with reference to the data, and then make tailored application recommendations. It increased users' positive feelings and satisfied their demands to the greatest extent possible.

In 2013, the tycoons were only talking about big data; by 2014, they were actually competing. Whoever could generate profits from development in big data could acquire a more advantageous position. It was believed that the mobile strategies employed by Ma would lead others to create similar products and approaches, providing users with more choice and facilitating the development and prosperity of the mobile internet market as a whole.

THE MARCH TOWARDS ANIME

In 2014, Tencent hosted the annual news conference for interactive entertainment. During the news conference, Tencent Anime made public its new strategy: to build an anime industry chain. In order to ensure the proper function of the industry chain, Tencent had already begun its first project – an official Naruto (the popular Japanese manga) fan website.

This was a strategic breakthrough for Tencent. Not only did it constitute a brand new experiment, it also provided anime fans with a good entertainment base. Over the past few years, the state had been supportive of the anime industry, giving it bright prospects. By building up the anime industry chain, Ma considered anime to be Tencent Entertainment's new battlefield. It was a large market, and the culture surrounding anime was hugely popular.

Ma primarily focused on the following four aspects: firstly, and most importantly, striving to produce good work for the fans. Secondly, it was important to strengthen the animation to spread its influence further. The third aspect involved strengthening the games themselves, and the fourth area of focus was upon strengthening related products to ensure the content could be further developed.

In 2014, the development plan devised by Ma for Tencent anime relied on the powerful platform Tencent had already constructed. It was a pan-entertainment strategy, intended to reorganize the Chinese anime industry so that a complete industry chain, revolving around popular concepts, could be established.

Not only would Ma introduce famous anime which were already popular, he would also develop original work in order to attract more fans to the Tencent anime community. *Shi Xiong*, a manga created by Qi Duyu, gained wide recognition after being published on Tencent Anime. With support from Ma, this manga had facilitated anime spin-offs, as well as offshoots related to gaming and other products. After his cooperation with Tencent Anime, Qi Duyu had become an artist who made millions every year.

At one press conference, Ma officially raised his new updated pan-entertainment strategy. People gradually became clearer about this new concept, which represented the symbiosis of the online world and mobile internet. With the support of this multi-industry platform, the Tencent business chain could be further developed.

Ma would henceforth be able to provide users with a good entertainment experience. He planned to spare no effort in his commercial strategy of introducing and developing popular intellectual property works to satisfy Tencent users' entertainment demands.

READING IS KING

In 2013, Tencent Literature, a subsidiary of Tencent Holdings, introduced the 4.0 Android version of QQ Reading. According to an official announcement from Tencent Reading, although the Chinese internet had experienced microblogs and games, the next battlefield would be in the mobile reading area. Tencent Reading would be gradually connected to Tencent's other social platforms. In relation to the details of the connection, Tencent was still planning and experimenting.

Ma had seen the future development of people's reading, and had strengthened Tencent's digital reading platform. Given the current status quo, the new version of QQ Reading was evolving in different directions: the content was richer; the functions were stronger; the visuals were healthier; and the details were better suited to the user's operation. Ma had also strengthened his cooperation with Chuangshi Chinese in order to provide reading content for the users.

In the second half of 2013, Tencent hosted a press conference in Beijing to officially launch its Tencent Literature brand name, business structure and full literature development strategy. During this important conference, Tencent Literature announced its business structure, which covered Chuangshi Chinese, a male-oriented original works website, and Yunqi Shuyuan, a female-oriented original works website. Apart from these two sites, it also included digitally published books sale platforms and PC gateways to Tencent Literature. Of course, Ma did not forget the mobile version: Tencent Literature also included a wireless gateway and a mobile version of QQ Reading.

The reason for the conference was primarily related to the mobile QQ Reading Centre. As its name suggested, the QQ Reading Centre was a platform based on QQ Reading. Its primary focus was light reading on social networking sites. If compared with the prior Tencent Game Centre, a significant change was that it would be promoted on the 'trends' area of the new mobile QQ.

One could tell from this that Ma had devised a full literature strategy based on a newly established business system. The system's rich content covered an entire industry chain, including the content and the users.

This huge structure had many obvious advantages. Firstly, in terms of the content, Tencent Literature covered both traditional and online works. By cooperating with its digital publishing platform and hundreds of publishers, it had formed a new strategic relationship that would advance online reading, without forgoing the promotion of traditional literature. In addition, Tencent Literature had also taken a huge progressive step in terms of user structure. It would provide its services to all QQ users, regardless of their age, gender or occupation. Such personalized service standards helped Tencent integrate all of its PC and mobile gateways. The biggest advantage of the integration was that all the books' content, reading progress and user data could be updated concurrently, in order to ensure the user could read the most updated content on the mobile version.

In order to guarantee the quality of the work, Ma established the Tencent Literature Consultants Group, which consisted of the Nobel Prize winner Mo Yan and other famous authors such as Alai, Su Tong, and Liu Zhenyun, among others.

Ma did not focus only on literary contacts, however. Tencent also formed cooperative relationships with filmmakers such as the Huayi Brothers Media Group, aiming to transform successful works of Tencent Literature into movie projects.

Ma's new strategy in the reading area was essentially a brand new organization of Tencent's industry chain. By making use of the pan-entertainment strategic concept, he could perfectly integrate new structures within Tencent's internet business, building a holistic structure which revolved around intellectual property authorization of games, films, TV shows and anime.

12 CHAPTER

THE
INNERMOST
WORLDS OF THE
PENGUIN EMPIRE

THE SECRETS OF MA'S RETIREMENT

On 15 February 2006, Ma resigned from his position as CEO. Liu Chiping who had previously worked as the strategic investment officer, took over Ma's role.

Ma explained the reasons behind the change: "In the past year, Mr Liu has contributed to our daily operation and management quite a lot. He is an important member of our management team. With Liu and his team's assistance, I will be able to put more energy into devising strategy and directions for the company and our products, providing better services to our users, while grasping the potential opportunities of the market."

Liu was indeed a very capable individual. By the time he was 25, he had received a Master's degree from Stanford and Northwest University. In addition, he had more than ten years' experience in stock issuance, M&A and management consultation. His only shortcoming was his unfamiliarity with instant messaging software. Liu used to be the executive director of the investment bank department in Goldman Sachs Asia, and first executive officer of its telecommunications and technology industry team. He had also spent some time working for McKinsey & Company in management consultation. From 2005, Liu began his job as the first strategic investment officer for Tencent, focusing on the guidance of strategy, investment and M&A. During this period, Tencent's stock price rose from ¥6 to more than ¥20, becoming the most valuable internet company in China.

Under Liu's control, the 'online life' strategy of Tencent had been fully enforced and had gradually progressed into instant telecommunications, online games, gateway websites, and even online businesses.

From Liu's point of view, 20% of a good enterprise depended on its strategy, and the rest was reliant upon the executive capacity of the company. It was exactly for this reason that Liu was determined to join the company, hoping to transform himself from an observer of the company's strategy, into an enforcer.

In 2005, Tencent changed its logo. At that time, the media opinion about this transformation was that it was merely a way for Tencent to celebrate the New Year. Ma would have to face new challenges as he changed roles and, in 2006, he explained that he believed the change of icon was a way for Tencent to expand its business. In so saying, Ma had revealed the truth: Tencent would continue to expand its business into areas beyond instant messaging (IM) software. Tencent had already realized some achievements in online gaming, gateway websites and online business areas, and had gradually transformed from a company making IM software to an online community company. At the same time, the employees of Tencent had increased to over 2,400, which presented new challenges for the company's HR department.

Ma understood clearly that Tencent would encounter new problems as it grew, and these problems would only be resolved properly if they could be diverted into different streams. With this knowledge, Ma had to focus his energy to push the penguin empire forward.

By resigning, Ma had also achieved another purpose: when a small company grows bigger, the leader's personal charisma will be less influential to the company's development as one individual's power is necessarily limited in order to remain effective within one particular stage of the company's development. When the company is bigger, what it needs is not to strengthen its personal power but transform from a model of individual heroism to a broader system of scientific management.

Ma's decision to resign related to his own character as well. Between 1998 and 2006, although Tencent had been expanding into new areas, it had been perfecting and regulating its existing services. It was the only company in China then to concentrate on IM software. In other words, instant communication has always been the focus of Tencent's business, and it would never be less important, even if other businesses were added. Essentially, this particular cultural system of being focused on the distinct area of IM software had gradually become part of Tencent's corporate culture.

Ma's resignation was intended to make Tencent into a community and a platform revolving around QQ, and to realize his grand strategy of an open internet. Users would be able to fully integrate their real life into their online life. This was no longer simply a concept: it was a matter of corporate spirit and faith.

TENCENT'S FIVE TIGERS NARROWED DOWN TO TWO

When Tencent was first established, the five founders had a relatively harmonious relationship. This was due to a reasonable distribution of interests and balance of power, and also owed much to their characters, which complemented each other. However, after some time working together, the founders encountered obstacles on each of their career paths. As a result, and harking back to the old adage that 'there is no endless banquet', three of the original founders left Tencent.

The first one to leave was Zeng Liqing, who began focusing on his investments. In 2007, Zeng officially resigned from his position in Tencent as COO, and became a lifelong honoured consultant for the company. The outside world speculated that the reason Zeng had left in 2007 was due to Liu Chiping's replacement of Ma's CEO position. Since Zeng used to be responsible for the daily operation of Tencent, if Liu became CEO, he would replace Zeng as well. As stated before, Zeng was sociable and extroverted, in stark contrast to Ma's more restrained character. Hence, considering the period of time the two worked together, it was inevitable that Zeng may have affected Ma's personal authority. Perhaps this was the reason behind Zeng's resignation.

Another founder of Tencent, Chen Yidan, left in March 2013, just as the company was issuing its financial report. Chen had been the CAO of Tencent since 1999, responsible for administrative, legal, human resources and charity work. Chen also dealt with matters related to intellectual property and government relations. During his 15 years at Tencent, Chen remained unobtrusive. Owing to Chen's proficiency in law, his contribution to Tencent – taking it from a small company to a globally famous large enterprise – was significant.

In Tencent, the general perception was that both Chen and Ma were the calm and considerate types. No matter what they did, they would always have a long-term plan. In addition to this, their skills complemented each other: Ma was outstanding in terms of products and technology, while Chen excelled in law and was able to quickly understand Ma's new ideas and strategies and provide practical advice.

Chen's resignation took place after talking with the other founders. Only after he had obtained their consent did he start to prepare for his resignation. After two years of preparation, waiting for the company business to become stable, he left. The manner of his resignation was typical of his composed and rational approach.

Similar to Chen, technology expert Zhang Zhidong was also an understated figure who barely had any public exposure. At Tencent, Zhang was entrusted with the role of executive director and CTO, focusing on developing patent technology for the firm, including the instant messaging platform and huge online application system. On 19 March 2014, when Zhang announced his resignation, many people within the company were disappointed.

QQ, which had been developed by Zhang, was now seen as a basic platform and therefore less important. WeChat, developed by Zhang Xiaolong, had become the new core of the business.

In addition, the online application system, which had previously been operated by Zhang Zhidong, had been replaced by newcomers. Zhang therefore felt that it was time for him to retire and to leave the future developments to the younger generation.

The job of the remaining founder, Xu Chenye, was to deal with issues in relation to the company funds, interactions with clients, and community and public relations. Interestingly enough, even though Xu was one of the founders, he was not a director, and was also one of the two founders who had the least shares.

Perhaps at the start of their entrepreneurship, nobody had considered resignation. However, it is inevitable that the passage of time leaves individuals with different experiences and priorities, and thus it was natural, that at various points, the founders chose different paths.

I NEED COPYRIGHT, TOO

After Tencent was sued by ICQ, patent and copyright issues became vitally important and Ma paid a great deal of attention to them. He knew that Tencent could not afford to make the same mistake again. In 2003, Tencent established an independent department – the Legal Department – to make use of the intellectual property law in protecting its interests. It recruited intellectual property rights researchers, lawyers and senior legal consultants.

The protection system built by Ma started from the beginning of all technology and product projects, as a tailored intellectual property protection strategy for each of them. In Ma's supply chain management system for new products, intellectual property rights evaluation was added before the product or new business was announced. In this way, they would be able to protect their new inventions from intellectual property rights infringements immediately.

After the creation of the new QQ icon, Ma sped up Tencent's protection over these artistic invention intellectual property rights, in order to avoid piracy.

Firstly, he worked on the common protection regime for commercial secrets and copyrights. Existing Tencent works, such as software codes and designs, were all to be covered by stringent protection measures. The aim was to keep their core commercial concepts and strategies secret, thus ensuring their competitiveness.

Next, he strengthened their copyrights and trademarks. In 2000, Tencent registered its cartoon penguin icon, one of their most important products. Tencent obtained full trademark registration for this, to prevent the theft of this much-loved image. At the same time, Tencent had put effort into protecting all of their core trademarks by applying for full trademark registration, forming a group of cartoon images centred on the penguin icon.

Finally, Ma confirmed the double protection strategy over patents and copyrights. Patent protection was managed by building a patent data management system and patent application tracing system; in this way, Tencent integrated their copyright protection and patent protection so that all applications were digitally managed. Through such steps, Tencent had become more systematic and regulated in its rights protection.

As Tencent received more and more benefits from intellectual property authorizations, Ma faced a new problem: how to efficiently manage the large number of rights. As is widely known, once an intellectual property right is authorized, the receiver enjoys total control over the right. If there is anything unclear in the contract, then the grantor may lose their say.

Ma gradually set up a QQ brand authorization model that fitted into Tencent's management characteristics. The model required that any product that used QQ's icon authorization, during the process of development, manufacture or sale, had to obtain Tencent's consent if the user wished to make any changes to the icon. All updated icons belonged to Tencent as intellectual property.

It may seem that Tencent's efforts to protect itself were merely reactionary after such a long period of ignorance. Actually this was an inevitable part of the company's development, and it simply happened to take place after the domain name lawsuit. It should be emphasized that Ma intended to protect Tencent's inventions by advancing his intellectual property strategies, as these would add value to

Tencent's brand name. This was the most direct way to gain financial benefits.

Ma had consistently proven himself to be capable of learning from failures. He did not indulge himself in frustration, but instead took the opportunity to discover hidden commercial opportunities. Combining creativity and technology, he made QQ into a famous brand name. It was precisely because he had lost the case that Ma became more aware of the intellectual property rights that now lay at the core of the company's competitiveness.

MA'S DOUBLE-BLADE

As the founder of Tencent, Ma has been dubbed the 'Father of the Penguin'. He certainly has many traits that can be found among many other successful business people. However, there are two particularly significant aspects of his character that have been crucial to the development of Tencent: his manoeuvering against competitors and his ability to grasp opportunities. These two principles became Ma's double-blade as he expanded the territory of the penguin empire.

Ma saw himself as a conservative man who did not favour taking risks. He used to say: "We will try some small innovation and experiments, but for bigger projects, like online games and online business, we will do some research first to know which of them are suitable for us. For example, if we think Taobao's model can bring out the advantages of a massive number of Chinese internet users, then our online business model will be inclined to learn from their model."

Ma recognized the importance of moving only after careful consideration. No matter what kind of decisions were made by Ma, he would first reflect upon how to synthesize the company's own learning cycle and the new industry's life cycle so that their project could progress smoothly.

Since the internet developed and evolved rapidly, it was often difficult to predict what would become popular. In this unpredictable situation, Ma had to be cautious and discreet as the leader of Tencent. It would be extremely costly if he ever made a wrong judgment, and so he had become more and more reluctant to be a pioneer. Instead, he hoped to rely on others' experience in considering whether he wanted to follow and learn from them before he entered the market. In this way, he could develop strong brand competition.

Although Ma preferred to strike later, he was good at grasping opportunities. Ma had said humbly in public many times that he was a lucky man because he had seized upon opportunities to make himself successful. Ma felt that his whole team, including himself, were not necessarily the smartest, but what they excelled in was grasping every chance that arose, and capitalizing upon it.

In 1995, Ma had first become aware of the internet, much earlier than many others. However it was certainly far from sufficient merely to know about the internet. One had to be sensitive to the overall development of the entire online world. Ma has shown himself to be exactly this type of man, possessing the strong technology acumen necessary to make the right commercial judgments, in order to predict future market trends.

His strength lay in his ability to make use of all the opportunities around him and create conditions to capture these chances. For instance, when there was a lack of computer experts, Ma made use of the geographical advantage of Shenzhen in order to seek talent and finance.

Apart from this, Ma possesses another skill for seizing upon potential opportunities. Before he makes any decision, he always considers every detail before becoming too deeply involved. Ma's pragmatism differentiates him from commercial gamblers, who recklessly bet everything they own. On the contrary, with meticulous consideration, he is able to put investors' hearts at ease with his commercial plans.

It is precisely because Tencent has grasped so many opportunities in internet development that it has risen to become the unquestionable king of instant telecommunications. It was Tencent who moved early to capture hundreds of millions users. Thus, the penguin empire grew stronger and stronger as its popularity and advantage became more and more significant. All of this should be attributed to Ma's wisdom in recognizing and grasping opportunities.

Owing to Ma's strategy of seizing opportunities, many competitors lost out to Tencent. As times change, so do technologies. From the internet to the mobile internet, from the PC to cell phones, the little penguin has experienced and grown through profound technological and cultural revolutions. Though the future may be unpredictable, the penguin empire will continue down its path of success towards its next victory, through the core value of 'communication'.

POSTSCRIPT

A SPEECH DELIVERED
BY MA HUATENG

CONTINUOUS RENEWAL IN THE 'INTERNET +' AGE

Distinguished Director Ren, Academician Li and Wu, Deputy Mayor Chen, distinguished guests, welcome to the 'Internet+summit'! My colleague has told me that there are over 800 government officials, experts, partners, and journalists present today. My colleague also told me that it was extremely hard to get a ticket for the summit this morning, which made him change his WeChat name to 'ticketless'. But we are still going to have another four forums this afternoon to allow more friends to arrive, and thus we value the current opportunity to talk to everyone here.

I remember, as the host just said, that we announced the executive agenda for the 'Internet+' summit at the 'Two Sessions' held last year. After more than a year's preparation, we have more Internet+ achievements to report.

Last year, I used the idea of industry revolution as a metaphor for Internet+. For example, we experienced the first and second industrial revolutions with the age of steam and electricity; now this is the third industrial revolution, powered by information. If we treat the internet as a power source for industry, then I think it should be clear that the internet is essential for industrial development.

In the past year, several important areas – like telecommunications, finance, retail, online to offline (O2O) and traffic – have experienced significant changes. I wish to share with you some of my observations.

Take the conventional telecommunications area, where operators have already embraced new internet communications like WeChat. The whole industry has transformed, from consuming voice mail and texts to consuming data.

But we have also seen, during the past year, the social problems that can arise in this area, like the spread of illegal and harmful information that can occur due to the large volume of data transmission. We feel a strong sense of responsibility and pressure in relation to the security of the information transmission process. We also plan to crack down on illegal gambling on the platform.

Online finance has developed smoothly. However, there has also been lots of illegal fundraising occurring under the name of online finance. This requires special attention.

We don't even need to mention O2O. Many of the people present here are our partners and are successful in integrating online and offline businesses. In the past year and a half, the entire O2O business of China has undergone massive changes, whether it be www.58.com or Meituan and Da Zhong Dian Ping. Many new opportunities have also arisen, like the integration of Xie Cheng, Qu Na'er and Yi Long in the travel industry.

Regarding 'Internet+ traffic', we have seen competition and integration between Didi and Kuaidi and their year-long competition with Uber, as well as major challenges from a policy-making perspective. For example, how does the 'Internet+traffic' model face the conventional taxi, and resolve the regulative and policy-making issues in this area? How do we deal with these conflicts?

While talking to Prime Minister Li Keqiang at a big data meeting in Guizhou, I provided bold advice while comparing ourselves with Alibaba: say if, ten years ago, a small shop owner on Taobao was outlawed for his lack of a business licence or inability to provide receipts, then we may not have Alibaba today; if, five years ago when We-Chat was created, we shut it down simply because it had challenged the existing operators, then we would not have the current WeChat market. The Prime Minister agreed with me and said we should give these new things a second look. Regarding those problems that emerge during the development process, we need to figure out a solution. In the age of Internet+, we have encountered enormous challenges and difficulties.

Over the past year, we have made considerable progress in the city and public service areas, with strong support from government at all levels. I have been to more than ten provinces since last year to promote the Internet+ model. I have also taken part in many seminars to introduce this concept and its benefits to officials. Over the past year, we have seen great progress in public security, taxation, and many other areas, including medicine and education. We also have seen many creative new companies. We have made new partners in related areas, many of whom are present here.

I believe there will be many new opportunities in the Internet+ age. What Tencent should and should not do is very clear in the current environment. We are the connector, and we hope to connect service providers with customers and open up the massive data owned by the government. Actually, for the past decade, the government at all levels has already stored up a large amount of data – there is a broad foundation for us to develop.

First is the cloud storage service. Tencent has always been quite strong in this respect. However, in the past, we only focused on our inside industry and department system, which was not separated and kept open. This year, we will completely open up our capacity in this respect and commercialise it at the same time. It will be wrapped up as our product and offered to society, government, and our partners.

The second is the geographical information or location based services (LBS). LBS is a vital part of the future mobile internet. It is not a business or profit-making business in itself. Tencent has invested in maps. We are cooperating with our partner Didi, which manages more than 10 million rides every day with live traffic data and the amalgamation of millions of cars' location information. We are also working with Jingdong's who produce millions of daily deliveries and delivery information. All these partners are producers and users of LBS, let alone Meituan and www.58.com, which has tens of thousands of shops around the country. Even those small takeout and express delivery services can all share location information down to the smallest lane. It is an unprecedented infrastructure.

Third, our focus on security. For more than five years, we have spared no effort or cost when investing in security. In the age of mobile internet, our mobile security services have been recognized across the industry. Just two days ago, Apple granted Tencent the only security service recognition on WWDC, making their official recommendation to users based on Tencent mobile manager's harassment interception function. This is an extremely important recognition for China and the Tencent security team. In the future, we can filter spam texts and marketing calls directly on Apple smartphones. It was impossible in the past. We have many other areas that require infrastructure of this kind, including payment services.

Last year, I mentioned that we hope to work with the Economic and Information Committee in order to be able to collect information from all industries and around the country. It will be a driving force in promoting the development of Internet+.

The huge amount of data, including public accounts, already provides information from every industry. But we still find it insufficient. Therefore, we have communicated with tycoons individually through WeChat: people like Liu, Yao, and Wang Xing. I asked them whether they can share their retail, online business, traffic and O2O data. Last year, we were in different cities and talked about whether we could integrate our data, and generate a full picture GDP through intelligent weighted analysis.

At first I thought it might not be possible, because I was worried about the reliability of such data. However, after several months of effort, now I think our team will be able to offer results. Nevertheless, I wish that, in the future, we can make it more real-time in presentation, and see live changes every day.

I will not occupy any more of your time, since there will be four more forums this afternoon, plus my team will present more about the Internet+ index later.

To finish, I hope that this summit proves fruitful, and that the guests presented can contribute more good ideas to all of us. Thank you everyone.